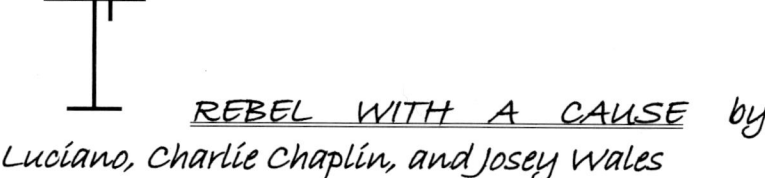

REBEL WITH A CAUSE by Luciano, Charlie Chaplin, and Josey Wales

This song is no joke Lovey. Death have not begun to take fully yet.

The Wicked and Evil; Children and People of Death have not fully started yet.

<u>Covid -19 is just their prerequisite for Genocide; the Mass Death that is to happen here on Earth greater than any death you've seen before. Allelujah</u>

Thus, humans especially those in the Black Race cannot see just how unjust and unfair the White Race is unto them, and others.

Death's Children and People write unjust and unfair laws to Shackle and Chain Blacks to their System and Systems of Death. Thus, no one Globally is safe from the Children and People of Death.

The Different Governments of the Different Black Lands refuse to kick Whites out of their land and lands. Whites that take control of it all. Therefore Lovey, we have to secure our land and lands, and Children and People from the Predators of Life – the

DARKNESS – BOOK TWO

White Race of Demons; Death that live amongst us here on Earth.

<u>Bob Marley did tell us; Blacks the truth in his songs, and it is us as Blacks that refuse to listen.</u>

It is us as Blacks that built the different civilizations.

We as Blacks that had higher knowledge.

Higher education.

Higher life, and look at the cost when we as Blacks trusted the White Race of Liars and Demons.

Listen to the lyrics of this Song (Crazy Bald Head) Black People because, Bob Marley was correct. <u>You were the ones to not listen to the truth. Therefore, Bob Marley, Marcus Mosiah Garvey, and more became the Jesus of your Bible. Not one of you listened to them, nor did anyone of you adhere to the truth and knowledge you were getting</u> thus, <u>YOU AS BLACKS CRUCIFIED THE TRUTH OF LIFE, AND THE TRUTH OF LIFE YOU WERE GIVEN.</u>

You as Blacks kept your foolish and unwise ways.

You as Blacks deceived yourself.

Now listen to <u>**CRAZY BALD HEAD**</u> by Luciano and Beene Man. Yes, same song by Bob Marley *with a different twist because; right now,* <u>*IT'S US AS BLACKS THAT ARE LIVING AS THE DECEIVED.*</u>

<u>*YOU AS BLACKS YOUR OWN BLACK DEMONIC LEADERS ARE KILLING AND KEEPING DOWN WITH THEIR UNJUST LAW AND LAWS.*</u>

<u>*YOU AS BLACKS THAT YOUR OWN BLACK DEMONIC LEADERS KEEP OPPRESSED AND SHACKLED AND CHAINED TO THE WHITE MAN'S WAY OF EVIL AND LIES; DEATH.*</u>

<u>*YOU AS BLACKS THAT YOUR OWN BLACK DEMONIC LEADERS SHAME AND ABUSE WHILE THEY KISS THE ASS OF THEIR WHITE COUNTERPARTS BECAUSE, THEY HAVE NO BLACK BONE OR BACK BONE LITERALLY.*</u>

<u>*Trust me, your wails have not yet begun.*</u>
Therefore, listen to the song <u>**REBEL WITH A CAUSE**</u> *by Luciano, Charlie Chaplin, and Josey Wales. You will see and know.*

The Children and People of Death did fulfill Death's Book; man's so-called Holy Bible.

<u>*It's not over Black People because, you will not be saved in it all and rightfully so.*</u> *You did not listen and adhere to the truth God for whom I call Lovey gave you to save you from what was, and is to come. All*

Blacks have and has forgotten, <u>***then; expect God to bow to your will by BOWING DOWN TO DEATH BY SACRIFICING LIFE UNTO DEATH FOR THE LOTS OF YOU.***</u>

GAD ANNO PUPPUNENNAY FI BLACK PEOPLE.

<u>Blacks will be destroyed</u> *thus, my different dreams I told you about in other books about the destruction of Blacks. Therefore, it's time for Blacks to stop deceiving self and look into the truth of Black History before the different races came into being.*

<u>WHITE HISTORY IS NOT BLACK HISTORY.</u>

<u>THE HISTORY YOU ARE GIVEN BY BLACK AND WHITE DEVILS IS NOT THE HISTORY AND TRUTH OF BLACKS.</u>

Now think and think truthfully, carefully, honestly, and clean, and tell me.

<u>WHY OUR BLACK GOD WAS WRITTEN OUT OF OUR LIFE, HISTORY, DNA, TRUTH, AND MORE?</u>

<u>WHAT DID WHITE AND BLACK DEVILS HAVE AND HAD TO GAIN OTHER THAN</u>

DARKNESS – BOOK TWO

THEM SENDING THE LOTS OF YOU TO HELL?

Think about it while I continue on with this book.

ONWARDS I GO

As we are in present day. Think Artificial Intelligence because, **this avenue will KILL YOU AND THEIR CREATORS LITERALLY.**

No Lovey, I truly do not want to be in Canada in the next year and a half. The 42 months of Revelations is almost up and still, humans have not put it together when it comes to Covid -19 and the Bullshit of Covid – 19, **and the DIFFERENT VACCINES THEY ARE FORCED TO TAKE.**

Blacks have not secured self with you Lovey.

Blacks Globally are still governed by White Laws, and the White Way of Living and Thinking.

Allelujah, I know, I know, I know Lovey. Therefore, many Blacks lack Higher Knowledge. Knowledge that will set them free.

Yes, the Slaughterhouse of Death where Blacks will be persecuted and slaughtered more shortly because; the White Race of Demons did not prepare a place for them in their so-called New World Order, and New Earth.

DARKNESS – BOOK TWO

Blacks refuse to align self; unite with each other truthfully, and peacefully. Instead, they fight against self, dirty self, dirty land, and dirty others to stay chained to Death.

<u>When we as Blacks take our Black God out of our life, all we are left with is Death.</u>

Right now, every human here on Earth have and has gone against God.

Listen to me. Hell is not the place to go or be in.

Every human has and have racked up so much Sin without knowing, some Sins are truly not forgiven.

Each Sin come at a cost to your Earthly and Spiritual Life, and more.

Allelujah Lovey. I truly do not want to be anyone Black; the left behinds come 2022, and beyond.

Now let me ask everyone in the Black Race based on hue this.

*Have we as Black People come this far from Lovey; our Black God to live as beings without a <u>**BLACK AND BACK BONE; SHAME?**</u>*

<u>Have we fallen this far from Lovey; our Black God that, we truly do not know who we are literally?</u>

DARKNESS – BOOK TWO

Yes, a stupid question on my part given the State of Blacks Globally, but what have we truly become in your eyes Lovey?

We lost everything including our Intellect and Home with you Lovey.

Blacks truly know not you.

Blacks have and has forgotten about you.

Blacks say they are Blacks but, are we truly; when we are brainwashed Psychologically, Socially, Educationally, Economically, Environmentally, Mentally, Religiously, Family Wise, our Black History Wise, Health Wise, Water Wise, Food Wise, Morally, Roots Wise, Culture Wise Lovey, and more?

Look at Blacks Lands how they've been colonized by the different demons that use land and people as their Whores and Prostitutes while robbing land and people of their wealth, life, moral values, and dignity.

Look at how Blacks massacre their own Blacks in the land and lands they live in.

Look at how Blacks hate Blacks especially if you speak to them truthfully, and without the need and needs including, want and wants of Religion, and Religious Lies.

Tell me truthfully Lovey. <u>How many Blacks will accept you?</u>

How many will acknowledge you Lovey as God, the truth of life, their saving grace, bank account of life, and more?

How many acknowledge their Sin and Sins here on Earth Lovey?

How many think about their Spiritual Well Being Lovey?

Look how many Blacks globally who believe in, and practice evil means to stay afloat here on Earth. Thus, Many Blacks have and has sacrificed self for Nastiness; all they were given and taught.

Come on Lovey, Blacks are truly lost because; **NONE KNOW WHERE TO TRULY BEGIN.**

WHY SACRIFICE *by Luciano and Natty King*

Africans aren't telling the truth. Africans are riding on and off the Coattail of Death to keep the rest of the Black Populace Globally enslaved; shackled and chained to Death. Slavery

An ounce of Black Knowledge is worth more than its weight in Gold Lovey come on now.

*With Black Knowledge; Truth, we will become unstoppable. Therefore, **BLACKS DID CONQUER BLACKS.***

DARKNESS – BOOK TWO

<u>BLACKS DID ENSLAVE BLACKS.</u>

<u>BLACKS DID LIE TO BLACKS.</u>

<u>BLACKS DO KEEP DEATH ALIVE.</u>

<u>BLACKS DID KEEP THEIR BLACK GOD FROM BLACKS.</u>

See:
African Lies.
Blacks lacking Unity.

Blacks lacking Black Knowledge.

Blacks lacking Truth.

Blacks lacking their own Black God.
Blacks being engrained in White Lies.

Blacks being engrained in Darkness. Voodoo and Obeah

Blacks being educated wrong about Blacks, and more.

<u>Therefore, BLACK DEATH CANNOT WALK AWAY FROM WHITE DEATH. BLACK DEATH MUST SERVE; DO AS WHITE DEATH SAY.</u>

So yes, certain things I know and comprehend Lovey but in truth, the failings and failure of Blacks on a whole truly do not make me feel any better.

The Lack of Unity and True Unity on the parts of Blacks truly do not make me feel any better.

Why be Slaves to Whites here on Earth to go to Hell and be a Slave to Death, the Demons of Hell, and the Pain you will feel in Hell for your Sins and Disobedience here on Earth?

Sadness right now is not in my vocabulary for Blacks Lovey. <u>I am still at a loss to our failings; THE FAILINGS OF BLACK PEOPLE.</u>

Lovey, do you think of Technology?

Lovey, humans especially those in the White Race are so barbaric that you have to wonder where civility went when it comes to them.

<u>No Lovey, did civility flee from this race and say, no; "I refuse to have anything to do with this race due to their barbaric nature?"</u>

Lovey I am sorry, but I had to ask that question.

<u>Come on Lovey. The Technology of White People is not True Technology. Their Technology is a death trap onto others. If they are not spying on people,</u>

<u>*they are finding, developing, and implementing ways to kill. Allelujah*</u>

Lovey, they make everything to kill. <u>**ONE DROP**</u> by **Bob Marley** because; the White Race did make this world so hard that people are fighting each other, and more.

<u>"ALL FOR THE WHITE RACE IS DEATH LOVEY COME ON NOW."</u>

Look how they war with other nations including self.

Look how they develop and manufacture weapons, diseases, nuclear weapons, viruses, and more to kill Lovey.

Warmongers are they from the past until now including, tomorrow.

Now they've come up with something called Artificial Intelligence. Now tell me Lovey, <u>"WHAT PURPOSE WILL ARTIFICIAL INTELLIGENCE SERVE APART FROM DEATH; THE WHITE RACE EXTENDING AND CONTINUING TO ASSERT THEIR MURDEROUS WAYS AND TENDENCIES HERE ON EARTH?"</u>

<u>"WHAT HUMAN IS SAFE HERE ON EARTH LOVEY WITH WHITE PEOPLE AROUND?"</u>

DARKNESS – BOOK TWO

No one can live in peace and true peace with this race around Lovey come on now.

You and I both know that; "**THE LEGACY OF WHITE PEOPLE IS DEATH.**"

THEY LIVE TO LIE.
LIVE BY THEIR ENTITLEMENT
LIVE TO DECEIVE
KILL

And if I am being Racist and Wrong Lovey truly forgive me.

Now I ask you this Lovey as it's December 8, 2021, and I started this book a while now.

I toggle between book one and two on some days.

WHAT RIGHT DO WHITE PEOPLE HAVE HERE ON EARTH?

WHY IS IT THAT BLACK PEOPLE CANNOT WAKE UP TO THE TRUTH, AND SEE AND KNOW THE TRUTH?

WHY DO BLACK PEOPLE KEEP DUMBING THEMSELVES DOWN?

DARKNESS – BOOK TWO

<u>WHY IS IT THAT BLACK PEOPLE CANNOT RECOGNIZE AND SEE THAT THEY ARE THE ELIMINATED RACE?</u>

<u>ONE IN THE BLACK RACE CAN SAVE THEM, AND THE WHITE RACE FROM THE CONCEPTION OF PROCREATION HAS AND HAVE BEEN TRYING TO ELIMINATE BLACK PEOPLE ESPECIALLY, THAT ONE SAVED. THEY THE WHITE RACE AND YES, THE DIFFERENT RACES WANT AND NEED BLACK PEOPLE TO FAIL THEREFORE, THEY DO ALL FOR BLACKS TO FAIL LITERALLY, AND WE AS BLACKS ARE HELPING OUR ENEMIES TO ELIMINATE US.</u>

<u>Our enemies know the power of Blacks.</u> How powerful we can, and will be as a true united force as well as, collective of people.

They; our enemies, know one in the Black Race can stop all facets of Evil and Death. Therefore, all that is false in given to Blacks so that they cannot succeed Physically and Spiritually.

<u>THE JOB OF ALL EVIL IS TO ENSURE BLACKS FAIL; YET, BLACK PEOPLE CANNOT</u>

<u>SEE THIS.</u> Nor is Africans telling the truth of Black Genealogy; Civilization.

<u>BLACKS GO ALONG WITH DEATH GLOBALLY WITHOUT KNOWING THAT ONCE BLACKS FAIL; SUCCESSORSHIP OF LIFE FALL IN THE HANDS OF THE CHINESE AND OR, MONGOLIAN RACE.</u>

<u>BLACKS WOULD HAVE FORFEITED LIFE WITH GOD, AND BLACKS ARE DOING THIS TODAY DUE TO SIN, RELIGION, EDUCATIONAL LIES, GENERATIONAL LIES, LIES OF TRADITION, AND MORE.</u>

So now tell me Lovey. How do any Black Person want and need life with you when they forfeit Life? Have and has given their life over to Death here on Earth.

Come on Lovey. Blacks are no longer leaders but followers; scavengers begging Bread off the White Man's Table. See Economy, Education, Sociology, Biblical Lies, and more.

We are not a people of honour anymore.
We are not a people of pride anymore.
We are no longer true Spiritual Beings.

Are not Educated Beings, but Caged Animals in the different Systems of Men; Death.

DARKNESS – BOOK TWO

We are not a people of You Lovey anymore come on now.

Life is given yet, many has and have taken their life and hand it over to Death literally.

Now, <u>**WAR IS INEVITABLE.**</u>

The White Race is gearing up to go to war from the looks of it to my dream this morning. This White Man dressed in white planting and or, positioning these blue things. So yes, more Death is coming; a lot more.

<u>Come on Lovey. As long as I am protected, the saved is protected, my family is protected, the truly trying to be good is protected, then I truly do not care how White People kill themselves literally.</u>

<u>They; Whites are not for me to save.</u>

<u>Those Blacks who fall under the White Banner of Death, are truly not for me to save, and I truly refuse to save those Blacks because; they are a true disgrace unto Black Life; You Lovey and Mother Earth come on now.</u>

F them. Let them die with Death because, it is Death that they serve. You don't give up your Black God for Fools Gold then want my God; the God of Life; True Life to save you. Have some damned respect for you, your culture, your race, your good and true upbringing, your good and true roots with your Black God, and more come on now.

Do not disgrace Black Life by going against Life period. Build your Life and Land truthfully. Come on now.

Represent Life because; <u>**BLACKS ARE THE TRUE CREATORS OF LIFE.**</u>

Do not downplay you as a Black Person.

God can't be doing all to save you, and you keep turning your back on God come on now. No Lovey, those Blacks who cry Crocodile Tears to you, let them walla inna dem dung literally. Hear them not because they are truly not Black. They are White as well as, <u>**LACK TRUTH AND LIFE.**</u>

<u>**STOP KILLING EACH OTHER AND START LIVING.**</u>

<u>**GOD DID MAKE US TRULY DIFFERENT FROM THE REST OF NATIONS THAT RESIDE WITH US HERE ON EARTH.**</u>

Many of you know the truth yet, use Religion as your base and defence to shatter, and kill your Black Own.

You lie on God with Religion. No wonder the White Race can use Blacks as their scapegoat globally.

DARKNESS – BOOK TWO

Africa is a prime example of this. And with all of this; <u>AFRICANS REFUSE TO LET GO OF THEIR WHITE AND DESTRUCTIVE WAYS</u>.

Therefore, Black Death is truly loyal to White Death. Nuh betta barrel nuh betta herring Lovey.

Now let's go back to technology Lovey because despite Man; Humans saying they are technologically advanced, they are <u>STILL BARBARIC AND WITHOUT LIFE, MORAL VALUES, AND RIGHTS.</u>

<u>Man's technology is not clean Lovey.</u>

<u>Man's technology was and is built on Death.</u>

<u>Man's technology will never ever help humans to attain good and true life because, those that built it; technology here on Earth, are truly not clean, nor do they have the best interest of life in thought, and what they are and were building. So no, humans cannot be trusted to do the right thing when it comes to life Lovey come on now.</u>

How can you design to kill?

Is it not the sick and demented who think Death is the answer to all life that are causing chaos here on Earth Lovey?

Is it not the sick and demented who think they can live for control and all that is evil here on Earth and bypass their death?

Is it not the sick and demented that think they can bypass Death here on Earth Lovey?

Is it not the sick and demented; delusional that think there are other planets out there that they can escape to, to bypass Death, and the ills they've done here on Earth Lovey?

Did no one tell them Lovey that; <u>ABSOLUTELY NO HUMAN; FLESHY CAN BYPASS DEATH IF THEIR NAME IS IN THE BOOK OF DEATH.</u>

Did no one tell them Lovey that; <u>ABSOLUTELY NO HUMAN; FLESHY CAN ESCAPE EARTH; LEAVE EARTH IN THE FLESH AND SPIRIT TO GO TO ANY FABRICATED PLANET.</u>

Did no one tell them Lovey that; <u>NO MATTER WHERE LIFE – YOU AS A HUMAN; FLESHY GO, DEATH GO(ES) WITH YOU.</u>

<u>ABSOLUTELY NO HUMAN; FLESHY HERE ON EARTH CAN TRAVEL WITHOUT LIFE AND DEATH.</u>

So yes; categorically yes. If I could write all evil and death out of life including, the DNA of Flesh and Spirit, I would do so for me, the saved of life; our good

DARKNESS – BOOK TWO

and true people Lovey including, the trying to be good.

Who the hell want or need evil around them day in and day our Lovey?

I don't thus, I petition you and get mad at you so.

The Saved and truly trying need to be delivered from Sin and Death here on Earth as well as, in the Spiritual Realm come on now Lovey.

The pang of hunger is taking fold Lovey; so, let me go get some breakfast and come back and write. Maybe not in this book but book one.

Have a safe and blessed day Lovey and think of me good and true. Open my mind and wisdom further truthfully because; I need Wisdom and Truth daily more than continually without end.

I need to save you and me Lovey. Smile

I need to save me and you. Smile

Oh, I so can't remember if I went back into the past via my dream world this morning but Lovey, if I did, <u>YOU HAVE TO PROTECT AND GUARD THE SAVED.</u>

<u>YOU CANNOT LET THE WHITE RACE OR ANY RACE DEVOUR THE SAVED.</u>

DARKNESS – BOOK TWO

THAT PERSON; THE SAVED HAS AND HAVE A JOB TO DO. TRULY LET THAT PERSON; THE SAVED BE VICTORIOUS OVER ALL WHO SEEK TO KILL HIM OR HER AS WELL AS, BE VICTORIOUS OVER ALL EVIL.

EVIL CANNOT WIN LOVEY. I REFUSE TO ALLOW YOU OR LET YOU LET EVIL WIN.

Now Lovey. IF MY GOODNESS AND TRUTH IS TRULY GOOD ENOUGH FOR YOU, THEN LET MY GOODNESS AND TRUTH BE ALL YOU NEED TO LET GOOD BE VICTORIOUS; YOU; US BE VICTORIOUS OVER ALL EVIL HERE ON EARTH AND EVERYWHERE EVIL RESIDES.

BE THE VICTORY I NEED AND WANT LOVEY COME ON NOW. LET IT ALL END WITH ME SO THAT DEATH CAN GO THEIR WAY IN TRUE PEACE AND HARMONY.

LET DEATH DIE – GO TO HELL WITH THEIR WICKED AND EVIL OWN TO LIVE OUT THEIR DAYS IN DEATH; AGONY.

And Lovey. No one in the Black Race can say they have not aided; helped Death in killing you; taking self from Life; You.

DARKNESS – BOOK TWO

None Lovey because, not even I can say this. Thus, the Sin and Sins of every man, woman, and child.

I refuse to lie to you Lovey come on now.

Hell is not my profit or prophet Lovey come on now. Good and true life is.

I need to gain good and true life not die in death, and with Death come on now.

Good and true life is worth it. It is humans that truly cannot see this, or respect life and the Law and Laws of Life.

Michelle

DARKNESS – BOOK TWO

Come on Lovey. <u>HUMANS DO NOT KNOW THAT THEY ARE THE ONES TO GIVE DEATH LIFE WITH THEIR SINS.</u>

<u>HUMANS TRULY DO NOT KNOW THAT; THE MORE THEY SIN IS THE LONGER DEATH STAYS ALIVE IN THE REALM OF DEATH, AND THE LONGER THEY BURN IN HELL.</u>

<u>HUMANS DO NOT KNOW THAT; ALTHOUGH THE FLESH DIES; THE SPIRIT CANNOT DIE HERE ON EARTH. HELL IS THE REALM OF SPIRITUAL DEATH WHERE YOUR SPIRIT HAVE TO PAY FOR ALL THE SINS; WRONGS YOU DO HERE ON EARTH IF YOUR NAME IS WRITTEN IN THE BOOK OF DEATH.</u>

<u>NO HUMAN CAN KILL THE SPIRIT OF MAN.</u>

<u>DEATH CANNOT SAVE LIFE LOVEY COME ON NOW.</u>

<u>IT IS HUMANS THAT HAS AND HAVE SAVED THE LIFE OF DEATH, AND THE CHILDREN AND PEOPLE OF DEATH FOR A TIME HERE ON EARTH.</u>

So yes; DEATH HAD TIME TO EXTEND THE LIFE OF DEATH DUE TO THE SIN AND SINS OF HUMANS.

Michelle

DARKNESS – BOOK TWO

Lovey, look at the Black Nations Globally; how the leaders sell out the land and people.

Look how the different nations use Blacks.

Cheat Blacks.

Use Blacks and their land as scapegoats to get money from people then, rob the land – that Black Land and their People of what was given to them via donations.

Look at me and how the Spiritual Wicked and Evil rob me of my Wealth here on Earth but, can never ever rob my Wealth and Truth of Me and You in the Spiritual Realm Lovey.

Blacks are demonized here on Earth and we as Blacks cannot see this; why?

<u>Come on Lovey, if we as Blacks found you yet again and live right and true; do you think any nation could bamboozle us as Blacks anymore?</u>

Come on Lovey, we would have found our place with you yet again, including, find the wisdom of life, the richness of life, life itself, and more would, and will flow through us in a good and true way.

<u>Blacks would dominate and become unstoppable, and this our enemies do not want or need.</u>

DARKNESS – BOOK TWO

When we know the truth and live by the truth; <u>DEATH WOULD CEASE TO EXIST.</u>

<u>DEATH'S CHILDREN AND PEOPLE WOULD COME TO AN END; LITERALLY DIE.</u>

Blacks are the Savours of Earth, and this Blacks truly do not know. Instead, we allow those Blacks that are loyal to Death take us from Life.

We allow the White Race and different races take us from life.

We allow our own Blacks to help us fail in Life and fail Life.

Blacks that take Life from their own Blacks.
Blacks that side with Death to kill us literally.

Blacks that get you as Blacks to sin reckless and rude.

Blacks Demons that show you and tell you it's okay to Bleach your skin.

Nasty Blacks that show you and tell you Polygamy; Whoredom is okay.

Nasty Blacks that show you and tell you the nastiness of Open Relationships is okay.

DARKNESS – BOOK TWO

Nasty Blacks and Black Demons that live in lies and deceit; whoredom. Their Islamic Way of Nastiness because; none know the True Islamic Way, or what Allah mean.

Blacks that have kids for this man and woman without knowing the consequences of their actions as they are giving Death extended life.

Blacks and Black Leaders that fail to tell you as Blacks the cost of each sin.

Africans – Blacks that lead you as Blacks blindly by keeping the truth from you.

Therefore, Blacks are not kind and civil to their own. Yes, not all but the majority because; <u>many have to KILL TO EAT TO THE SACRIFICES THEY MAKE UNTO DEATH.</u>

<u>THE OBEAH, SCIENCE, HUMAN AND ANIMAL SACRIFICES THEY MAKE UNTO DEATH, VOODOO; ALL THE EVIL THEY PARTICIPATE IN, AND DO.</u>

<u>THE NEGATIVE FORCES THAT SURROUND SOME THAT WHEN THEY COME AROUND YOU, THEIR NEGATIVE FORCES AND ENERGY LITERALLY WEAKENS YOU, AND TRAP YOU.</u>

DARKNESS – BOOK TWO

Yes, there is more but; I am going to leave it at that for now Lovey.

Therefore, Blacks have and has overlooked <u>STRIFE</u>. The beginning of Genesis where Whites lied on Life.

You Lovey did not put Strife between the Devil's Seed and Thy Seed come on now Lovey.

<u>Evil; Death's Children and People survive on Strife and Death</u> *thus, all they do is plant and or, put enmity in the hearts of humans thus, humans hate without a cause.*

Humans – Nations hate Blacks and will forever hate Blacks because; many in the Black Race is highly favoured by you Lovey come on now.

Blacks have limitless power this I know but, Blacks do not unify truthfully to exercise their right, rights, and power.

Many refuse to let go of Whites and the White Way of Life.

Many refuse to see self in life without the different races of haters.

Many refuse to let the different Races fall due to our caring and good will. Our good and caring ways that see many turning the other cheek, forfeiting life, disobeying life; You Lovey for the Ills of Death.

DARKNESS – BOOK TWO

When you give up Life you accept Death. You become like the dead, and many Blacks are dead literally.

Evil must fall.
Evil must end.

I am putting a stop to Death and Evil Lovey.

I refuse to let Death and Evil continue to reign here on Earth.

I refuse to let Death and Evil have more extension here on Earth, or anywhere for that matter.

It's time to let all who are wicked and evil go Lovey, and I've been telling you this for years.

<u>ROBOTICS IS THE DEATH OF HUMANS LOVEY.</u>

Humans are going to fully and truly die once Robots take full effect here on Earth. I know this for a fact without doubt.

<u>THE CONTROLLERS WILL BECOME THE CONTROLLED THIS I KNOW FOR A FACT TOO.</u>

<u>THEREFORE, MANY IN THE HUMAN POPULACE DESIGN AND CREATE TO KILL LITERALLY.</u>

DARKNESS – BOOK TWO

Due to White Control no one here on Earth hath a life.

Therefore, we need your help Lovey to overcome, and dismantle all the evils humans no matter the race and gender here on Earth has and have designed and created.

Thus, humanity I dedicate:

HEAVEN HELP US ALL *by Luciano to the lots of you because; without God, not one of you have life.*

All that is to come is going to further kill humans globally.

Man, humans <u>ARE BANKRUPT LOVEY; LIFE WISE.</u>

We as humans have and has bankrupt ourselves literally.

Without God; the True God of Life, you have nothing at all and in this case, nothing is truly nothing.

EVIL ISN'T GOD.

<u>EVIL IS/ARE HUMANS; ALL HUMAN BEING HERE ON EARTH.</u>

DARKNESS – BOOK TWO

SEE YOUR SIN AND SINS LITERALLY AND TALLY THEM UP, AND YOU WILL SEE YOU IN DEATH LITERALLY.

Wow, my head is hurting a bit.

I am going to get some water and lay down a bit. I have a two thirty phone appointment, but I don't think I am going to make it through the entire conversation to the way I feel right now.

Did I speak to my sister not too long ago?

Yes

And I am going to say this. As parents that want and need what's best for our children, we have to know when to let go of our children. We cannot continue to do our best raising ungrateful children that do not want or need to see your goodness.

Some of us as Black Parents do all the good for our children so that their future is bright and easy, and many of our children cannot see this; what we are doing for them. So, they create so much problem in your life, disrespect you, quarrel with you, hate you, and more. Therefore, we as parents have to learn when to let go of our foolish and unwise children that do not want or need the easy way in life.

I'm giving you the easy way. Latch on to the easy way, gain right and true that your future is easy and bright, but some Black Kids cannot see this. Work with that good parent uniformly and make a world that is harmonious, happy, true, good and clean for you in the future come on now.

Stop living in dysfunction because this is what the enemy need and want for all Blacks.

<u>THE AGENDA OF ALL OUR ENEMIES IN NOT TO SEE THE BLACK RACE SUCCEED. IT IS TO SEE THE BLACK RACE FAIL AT EVERY STEP AND CORNER, AND WE AS BLACKS HAVE AND HAS ALLOWED THIS TO HAPPEN; OUR ENEMY AND ENEMIES TO DEFEAT US, RAPE AND ROB US OF ALL THAT IS GOOD AND TRUE; RIGHT FOR US AND OUR LAND.</u>

Now:

LOOK AT BLACK OWNERSHIP GLOBALLY.

DO BLACK PEOPLE OWN THE DIFFERENT RESOURCES IN THEIR LAND AND LANDS?

DO BLACK PEOPLE BENEFIT FROM THE RESOURCES IN THEIR LAND AND LANDS?

DARKNESS – BOOK TWO

DO BLACK PEOPLE HAVE TRUE OWNERSHIP OF BUSINESSES YOU SET UP IN YOUR LAND TO HELP YOU AND YOUR FAMILY?

HOW MANY OF YOU THAT HAS AND HAVE SET UP SHOP IN YOUR BLACK LAND ARE BEING HARASSED BY THE DIFFERENT SCUMS THAT CALL THEMSELVES LAW INFORCEMENT OFFICERS IN YOUR LAND?

HOW MANY OF YOU ARE BEING EXTORTED BY YOUR OWN BLACKS INCLUDING, THE DEMONIC POLITICIANS YOU ELECT INTO OFFICE?

HOW MANY OF YOU ARE BEING RAPED AND MURDERED BY YOUR OWN BLACKS?

HOW MANY OF YOU FOLLOW BEHIND CORRUPT BLACK LEADERS AND HAS AND HAVE GIVEN YOUR LIFE OVER TO YOUR DEMONIC BLACK LEADER THUS, SOLIDIFYING YOUR PHYSICAL LIFE AND SPIRITUAL LIFE IN HELL LITERALLY WITHOUT YOU KNOWING THIS?

HOW MANY OF YOU AS PARENTS SELL YOUR CHILDREN INTO CHILD SLAVERY?

HOW MANY OF YOU AS PARENTS HAVE AND HAS SOLD YOUR CHILD AND OR, CHILDREN INTO PROSTITUTION?

HOW MANY OF YOU AS PARENTS HAVE AND HAS ABUSED AND KILLED YOUR CHILDREN?

HOW MANY OF YOU CARRY GENERATIOANAL CURSES WITH YOU EVERYWHERE YOU GO?

HOW MANY OF YOU AS PARENTS PRACTICE INCEST IN YOUR HOME THUS, DEFILING YOUR CHILD; CHILDREN?

See your Bible that from beginning to End. Thus, the beginning of Man – humans as given to you by the White Race of Demons and Liars is based on Incest – all that is nasty; unclean.

Therefore:

"THE NASTINESS YOU BELIEVE IN, IS THE NASTINESS YOU BECOME."

Michelle

DARKNESS – BOOK TWO

Black People truly need to look into self Lovey come on now. How can we have life when all around us is evil?

How can we live if, Death is what we are given to live by by our enemies come on now?

Lovey, as Blacks we are not letting you be our shield, sword, and rock come on now.

Life is not a belief.
Life is real.

Life is our good and true way to you Lovey come on now.

No one of Death can attain good and true life once the Spirit shed the Flesh, come on now.

<u>**Yes, we as humans punish self with our lack of knowledge.**</u>

We know no evil can tell the truth yet, as humans; we have wicked and evil people governing us as well as, leading us.

Lovey, you and I know that Evil lack truth.

You and I know the White Race lack knowledge, and truth. Hence, their Book of Death so-called Holy Bible of Lies; Sin, and Deceit come on now.

You and I know the White Race lack life.

DARKNESS – BOOK TWO

You and I know some in the Black Race lack truth.

You and I know some in the Black Race lack knowledge and true knowledge.

You and I know some in the Black Race lack life and true life.

In all we know Lovey, we cannot save all because; all is truly not of life.

Aye Lovey because there is so much that is left for me and you to do in my view.

I truly do not like the darkness Lovey, and I do not know why people would want or need to live in Total Darkness.

I see the Moon at nights and see the darkness that engulf some of its brightness, and I truly do not want or need this darkness for self, the saved, my family, and the truly trying to be good Lovey. Not even Mother Earth or You including, the Moon I want, or need this darkness for come on now.

I truly love you but that darkness Lovey wow. And I am going to leave things at that Lovey.

I do not know why humans cannot see the beauty of life.

Why do all that is sinful live to go to a dark place spiritually?

DARKNESS – BOOK TWO

Death's book – man's so-called Holy Bible is finished Lovey therefore, we need a new, good, and better way of life and living here on Earth without Death's Wicked and Evil Children and People come on now.

I need you beside me Lovey. You are my good and true stay and keep in life come on now.

THE WORLD IS TROUBLED *by Luciano*

Our New Earth cannot be troubled Lovey.

Our New Earth cannot have troubled children and people.

Our New Earth cannot have wicked and evil people and spirits in it Lovey come on now. We have a new slate and plate so, let's live good, clean, true, debt and death free come on now.

Aye Lovey we need to do a better job of sustaining and maintaining us here on Earth in a good and true way come on now.

I am going to see about walking Queenie and cook some food as it's 6:20 pm and it's truly dark outside.

Michelle

DARKNESS – BOOK TWO

Oh Lovey, this song; <u>ULTERIOR MOTIVE</u> by Luciano is so for you for real. This song tells of you in that; <u>HUMANS TRULY DO NOT LOVE YOU OR KNOW YOU.</u>

<u>Humans take you for granted and more.</u>

Now tell me:

How many people tell you that they love you but deceive you day in and day out?

<u>How many people that say they are Preachers, Pastors, Imams, Deacons, and more that say they are preaching on your behalf Lovey by teaching people about you, and rob and deceive their congregation, and the world?</u>

How many say they are leading your flocks to glory yet, murder those people?

How many of these religious demons that go into Black Lands and deceive the people, rape the people, use the people, steal from the people, and more evil things?

How many say, you have to give 10% of your earnings; wages to the Church yet, those that need help in and out of the Church live in abject poverty whist these Preachers live the life of luxury?

Not one cent of all the monies collected go into your Bank Account Lovey.

Not one cent of all the monies collected go into helping you Lovey yet, humans cannot see this. They still give falsely to Demons that Rape and Rob them of Life, and a place in your Kingdom and Domain Lovey.

Miss Martha down the road need help yet, these Church Leaders ignore her, have not truth, or the heart to help her. So now tell me Lovey, who is robbing who?

I know it's not you therefore, I know there is absolutely no home in your Realm of Truth for any Church Leader or Parishioner. Allelujah

Now Lovey; these Preachers say they are of you yet, have no Lovey, or God Bank Account with you.

<u>How many here on Earth Lovey truly love you and do the good they can not just for self, but for you, and the saved?</u>

*How many here on Earth Lovey say they <u>**LOVE YOU**</u> truly give you true thanks by; sitting upright in their chair, on their bed, on their sofa, while in the shower, cooking, washing the dishes, sitting on their toilet tell you thanks, or even send up to you true blessing of truth, and more?*

DARKNESS – BOOK TWO

How many say to you Lovey, on this day thank you for you. I do not need any blessing or blessings from you on this day. This is my way of thanking you, and showing you my truth and true love of you?

<u>How many dedicate their children in goodness and truth to you by saying Lovey, before I have children; please ensure that life that comes from me is of the good and true you, be born clean, true to life, obedient, smart, wise, free of sin and shame, dedicated to good and true life with you Lovey, ever growing up good and true, have no form of evil in their physical and spiritual DNA; makeup, and more?</u>

<u>Yes, Lovey I did not know this. Now that I know what qualities to ask you for in my children, I wish I could go back in time in the flesh to change things, and tell you Lovey of these qualities before I had all my children including, ask you for the right and good person; mate to lay with to procreate.</u>

Yes, I know about Creation. So, with all I know about Creation, we Lovey need to create good and true.

Yes, as my children are older now, I still have truth and hope in some way for all of them. Truly wish and hope as life move forward, they will come into their own, and see the goodness and truth of Life with you Lovey come on now.

DARKNESS – BOOK TWO

Aye Lovey, you are my truth and world. So yes, <u>ULTERIOR MOTIVE</u> by Luciano truly fit and suit you because; humans do lie to you, lie on you, take you for granted, do all to displease and dishonour you, take all life from you, and more wicked and evil things come on now.

Tell me Lovey; how can humans look to you for help when humans truly do not know you, nor can humans give you anything clean?

Lovey, do any of us as humans give to you clean?

I will not take myself out of this because; I am living amongst the unclean, and not all in my home is clean come on now.

I have to be fair and true to you Lovey come on now.

So Lovey, when will we go home together good and true; clean?

I have to reach the Southern Lands of Africa good and true with you. Jamaica is too unclean; dirty for me, and you will not let me go into Jamaica.

Jamaica is a forbidden Land for Me and You because; Jamaicans did take their Blessings from self with the filth they do out there. Therefore, no good and true home can be found in Jamaica. Yes, <u>Jamaica has become modern day Sodom and Gomorrah</u> this I know. <u>Jamaica is the land you deemed dirty; unclean here on Earth Lovey.</u>

DARKNESS – BOOK TWO

Jamaicans cannot blame anyone but self because; the heart and mind of them; Jamaicans is more than dutty and mucky. Too much Obeah, too much Science, too much badmine, too much death; killings, and more. Plus, the debts of that land have and has not been paid. Port Royal, and the sinking of Port Royal in June of 1692.

Yes, this is a shame because; I was born in that land, but I cannot save land and people because; <u>THEIR SINS DID OUTWEIGH THEIR GOODNESS LITERALLY.</u>

Hence, you Lovey deemed Land and People dirty; unclean.

So yes, another Black Land bite the dust due to the Wickedness and Evils of the People literally.

Luciano, Iba Mahr, and Chezidek <u>NICE & EASY RIDDIM MEDLEY</u>

Michelle

It's December 12, 2021, and man I kept dreaming about Da Brat.

So not going to worry about her and her relationship.

Something is so not right. There is no love or true love there in that relationship just coldness.

And no, I am not dropping stones, but the aura was that of coldness. As if there is no love or true love there and or, in that relationship.

Did I dream a Blue and White Sky with this beautiful light beaming though the clouds?

Yes

So do not know what Lovey and Mother Earth is telling me but, thank you both for the beauty and truth. I have to say, I am satisfied with the both of you for showing me such beauty and yes, comfort.

I asked for it; comfort, and I got it. Truly thank you Lovey, you did complete me in a beautiful way.

Michelle

DARKNESS – BOOK TWO

Yeah, it's nice outside and it's December 13, 2021.

The year is almost over. As for my dreams, wow.

Dreamt Serina Williams and her sister playing tennis in this Shopping Mall like complex. There is more to the dream, but I am so not going to get into this dream. I truly do not want to.

Don't really care for the Willams Sisters.

Never mind because.....wow.

Did I dream Shooting Stars?

I did, and I made a wish.

Did I dream about these little white balls?

Yes

This just mean more death is coming Physically and Spiritually that's all.

And that's it for my dreams; at least that I can remember.

Michelle

DARKNESS – BOOK TWO

For you the good and true and truly trying to be good, better must come and better do come. Although the road is rough; trust you, know you, hold firmly unto God. God is your victory no matter what.

Now I am going to send you to YouTube.

Bring up this song:

NEVER GIVE UP by Luciano

Yes, it's rough but joy cometh in the morning despite you saying, I doubt that. My pain is my pain, I'm the one feeling pain, it's me that is hungry, it's me that can't find food to feed my children, me that have financial woes, health woes, and more.

Listen, I know your pain, health woes, financial woes, and more.

Yes, I lash out at God, but I am not worse off.

Some of you are facing homelessness, but don't give up. Keep praying truthfully to God for a better and true way for you and your family.

Listen, God has made it so that I can pay my rent and bills despite me having a negative bank account.

You have Health Woes like me. I watch Chef Ricardo on YouTube at times, and he gives great health and healing tips.

DARKNESS – BOOK TWO

He said, Peppermint, Cinnamon, and Olive Oil mixed together will help your pain.

You have to crush the peppermint. I do not have Peppermint Leaves to crush. I had Organic Cinnamon and I had as well as, my daughter had cooking Extra Virgin Olive Oil, and I used some of hers; Extra Virgin Olive Oil and no word of a lie, the Olive Oil and Cinnamon helped me; my pain.

Trust me, I used some before I went grocery shopping for my dad as well as, travelling to my dad after doing his groceries, and stopping on the way to his house where I had to walk to get more groceries, and it truly helped me with the pain.

You have to try little things for you that help you.

You have to do your research. At times, well I am on YouTube too much, but it is where I will see little things and try it. Not all things. But know, God do lead you to different sources good and true.

If you truly love God and trust God, never stop talking to God. If you are angry, and you have that good and true; excellent relationship with God like I do, lash out at God so that God knows how you truly feel.

Listen, at times when I least expect it, I get things.

My older brother sent me a brand-new Winter Jacket last week that I use. Trust me, the Jacket is warm and nice. Food, I did not have to worry about all of

DARKNESS – BOOK TWO

last week because my son cooked, and before my daughter left for her mini trip in Canada, she would cook.

Personally, all I need I have. Now I am going to get a printer. The one I have is truly not working.

So no, I cannot give up on God. God is my good and true source and need, and I am telling you, <u>*"DO NOT GIVE UP ON GOD. GOD IS THERE FOR YOU."*</u>

Remember, God cannot fail you.

Those you trust and are true to you, will not fail you. Yes, some things they do will disappoint you, but true friends and true family will always be there for you.

<u>*"LET GOD BE YOUR GOOD AND TRUE FRIEND SO THAT GOD CAN SURPRISE YOU AND SPOIL YOU COME ON NOW."*</u>

Yes, your mind will egg you on to give up, but do not listen to the negative side of you.

Trust me, if there was a way to shut down the Negative Side of me, I would without hesitation.

People will tell you to give up, but don't give up on You and God.

Yes, you can take a break today, but get back on track tomorrow if you cannot go on today. <u>*But never give up on you.*</u>

DARKNESS – BOOK TWO

<u>Never give up on your abilities.</u>
<u>Never give up on God.</u>

If you want and truly love being a doctor. Let no one tell you don't be a doctor, or you cannot be a doctor. <u>It's your life and absolutely no one can live your life for you.</u> Your friend and friends cannot live your life for you. They were not born as you, and no one can be born as you; not even your twin if you have a twin.

Your true passion; love is yours therefore, stay on the path of righteousness when it comes to your true passion, and passion of being a doctor. Yes, you will have hiccups along the way, but never give up on your passion and true passions.

Do not look at the miles or years, go at your own pace and you will never ever fail.

Yes, one by one, step by step. Therefore, no one can pick fruits two at a time I don't think. But it matters not. One by one step by step you go.

Now if you have a bag a rice; cook some, and if you have a tin of sardine add some cabbage to that sardine if you have that tin of sardine.

Fry dumpling if you only have flour. If you have cabbage and tomato, steam the cabbage and tomato to go with the fry dumpling.

"<u>TEK YU HAN MEK FASHION" come on now.</u>

DARKNESS – BOOK TWO

Yu baggy ha hole inna eee.

Yu ha needle and thread, cut a piece of one of your ole frack an sew up yu panty.

Hey, mek a new fashion. Patch work baggy come on now.

Your mind is not limited therefore, <u>NEVER LIMIT YOURSELF TO THE NEGATIVES OF LIFE BECAUSE; THERE ARE SO MANY POSITIVES OUT THERE, AND IN YOU.</u> You just need a little push that's all.

Never forget, your life is your life.
Your parent's life is their life.
Your children's life is their life.
Your friend's life is your friend's life.

So, live good, true, and clean for you.

<u>UNITED STATES OF AFRICA</u> by Luciano

<u>I'LL LIVE AGAIN</u> by Beresford Hammond aka Beres Hammond

Michelle

DARKNESS – BOOK TWO

<u>REBEL WITHOUT A CAUSE</u> by Luciano, Charlie Chaplin, and Josey Wales

Truly listen to this song because, Luciano is correct on every level.

Listen to what he said about the rough times that is going to happen.

Is this not what is happening here now?

Covid -19 has and have taken the right and rights of every human from them globally.

You are not free to do as you like. Now think and tell me, <u>WAS THIS VIRUS CALLED FOR AND OR, NECESSARY?</u>

No Michelle, you should not ask that question because; <u>HUMANS GLOBALLY DID HELP DEATH TO FULFILL THE BOOK OF DEATH WITHOUT KNOWING IT.</u>

Death required 42 months; 3.5 years to enslave humans to devise their true Master Plan. <u>But, while evil was planning and scheming here on Earth; GOD WAS ENSURING NONE; NOT ONE EVIL PERSON COULD REACH THE REALM OF TRUTH; GOD.</u>

<u>GREAT DEATH AWAITS THEM ALL.</u> This I know for a fact without doubt.

Come on Lovey. Are humans not living their life without a cause; as the enslaved?

Are humans not living in, and fighting depression and poverty?

Job Loss – Joblessness; are hundreds of millions of you not facing joblessness?

Millions have and has been displaced.

Look at the homelessness. Many of you have and has been evicted from your homes because you cannot pay your rent.

Look at the Family Cost. How many of you have and has lost your family members to this virus and lie?

How many are now killing others and family members?

How many businesses worldwide have closed permanently?

How many of you have to be locked in your homes and hotels quarantining?

How many businesses are being looted right now?

DARKNESS – BOOK TWO

No one has seen that their Virus; Covid -19 Virus have and has totally destroyed billions of lives here on Earth.

Now tell me, <u>can any Evil Government, Evil Scientists, Evil Pharmaceutical Company, Evil Doctor, Evil Person compensate you for the life, and lives they've taken in the name of Greed and Death?</u>

Now tell me, are any of you consciously thinking about your life and what's to come?

Listen and tell me, <u>IF YOU HAVE NO VIRUS; HOW CAN YOU GIVE IT TO SOMEONE?</u>

<u>IF YOU HAVE NO GERMS, HOW CAN YOU GIVE THIS GERM TO OTHERS?</u>

<u>IS IT NOT THOSE WHO HAVE TAKEN THEIR VACCINE WITH THE VIRUS IN IT ARE THE ONES TO GIVE IT TO OTHERS; THIS VIRUS?</u>

Those who have the Vaccine are the Virus Carriers come on now. Think

Your brain is not limited yet, we as humans let others limit our thinking; dumb us down.

<u>CONTROL IS NOT THE ANSWER TO LIFE AND LIVING.</u>

DARKNESS – BOOK TWO

<u>*CONTROL IS SLAVERY PERIOD.*</u> *You are told what to do, when to do it, how to do it, how to think, how to lie and deceive, how to live, how to have sex, how to raise your family, and more.*

When you are controlled; <u>*YOU HAVE ABSOLUTELY NO LIFE OR RIGHTS.*</u> *Thus, Covid -19 did control you and billions whist taking your Humans Rights and God Rights from you. Revelations 13 fulfilled because, Billions of You had to take the Mark of the Beast.*

If you do not take the Mark of the Beast, you cannot:

Work
Buy as you like
Sell as you like
Walk as you like
Collect Unemployment Insurance
Go to School
Commune with your own family
Commune as you like with your friends

Some doctors refuse to see you because you are not vaccinated, and more.

Covid -19 did affect your Psychological Well Being.

Covid -19 did divide People and Nations.

DARKNESS – BOOK TWO

Covid -19 did put a divide between those who are vaccinated from those who are not vaccinated.

Our travel rights have and has been taken from us.

<u>OUR LIFE RIGHTS WITH SELF AND GOD HAS AND HAVE BEEN TAKEN FROM BILLIONS.</u>

Your fundamental Human Right and Rights have and has been taken from you thus, violating us as Humans and Spirit.

Oh yes, I did present my case with God.
I did cry to God.
I did cuss out God.

Therefore, <u>GREATER DEATH FOR THE DIFFERENT POLITICIANS OF THE GLOBE THAT FORCED DEATH – THE DIFFERENT VACCINES OF DEATH ON THEIR PEOPLE.</u>

<u>GREATER DEATH FOR EVERY SCIENTIST WHO PARTICIPATED IN KILLING BILLIONS BY DEVELOPING THIS VIRUS AND OTHERS.</u>

<u>GREATER DEATH FOR EVERY HUMAN THAT CONVINCE OTHERS TO TAKE THE VIRUSES – VACCINES OF DEATH.</u>

DARKNESS – BOOK TWO

GREATER DEATH FOR EVERY DOCTOR AND NURSE THAT HAS AND HAVE COMPLIED WILLINGLY AND KNOWINGLY TO GIVE PEOPLE THE DIFFERENT VACCINES OF DEATH.

GREATER DEATH FOR THEIR CHILDREN AND SOME FAMILY MEMBERS BECAUSE; MY TEARS DID GO UP TO GOD THEREFORE, THE CHILDREN AND SOME FAMILY MEMBERS IF NOT ALL MEMBERS OF YOU THE WICKED AND EVIL MUST GO TO HELL AND DIE.

GREATER DEATH FOR THE DIFFERENT PHARMACEUTICAL COMPANIES THAT DID PRODUCE AND MANUFACTURE THIS VIRUS AND THE DIFFERENT VACCINES.

GREATER DEATH FOR THE DIFFERENT SHAREHOLDERS OF THE DIFFERENT CORPORATIONS, AND EACH INDIVIDUAL EMPLOYEE THAT WORK FOR THESE COMPANIES WHETHER LIVING OR DEATH.

Trust me, DEATH DID BECOME RICH OFF THE LOTS OF YOU.

DARKNESS – BOOK TWO

<u>GREATER DEATH HAVE YOU ALL LOCKED IN HELL LITERALLY.</u>

<u>NOT ONE OF YOU ASSOCIATED WITH COVID -19 AND MORE CAN ESCAPE YOUR JUDGEMENT. YOU AUTOMATICALLY SEE – GO TO THE REALM OF GREAT DEATH ONCE YOUR SPIRIT SHED THE FLESH.</u>

<u>Oh. Worry not. Your children will be there with the lots of you. So, if your Child's Name was in the Book of Life, their name must be taken out of the Book of Life and put in the Book of Death thanks to you. And their name have and has been taken out of the Book of Life. This I know for a fact without doubt.</u>

<u>Your Sin and Sins; what you've done in the name of Death has and have recorded as well as, condemned the lots of you literally.</u> Cursed are the lots of you; every Political Leader, Boss, Employee of the different companies globally that develop vaccines with different viruses in them including, the Covid -19 vaccines, every Scientist that knowingly and willingly developed this virus Covid – 19 virus, and more, every doctor, nurse, and more that force people to take the different vaccines of Death, and more from generation unto generation more than

infinitely and indefinitely more than continually without end. This curse can never ever be lifted or broken.

Cursed must your children and their children be from generation unto generation more than infinitely and indefinitely more than continually without end.

"THOU SHALT NOT KILL." Do not force people to kill – die.

Cursed must your lands be for more than everlasting unto everlasting.

Earth must now close off her goodness unto your land and lands.

Due to Curse, every Political Leader, Boss, Corporation that develop anything to kill; for Death, Control, and more. Every Shareholder of the different Corporations of Death, every Owner of the different Corporations of Death, every Doctor, Nurse, Business Owner, Employee, and more that force their Citizens and others to go against their good and true Will to take the Vaccines of Death, you must now lose it all continually without end from generation unto generation. Financially you must be left in Ruin *never to ever rise ever again. Think of the People you've displaced and caused to lose it all financially, health wise, emotionally, God Wise, family wise, and more.*

For all you have and has killed in the name of Science, Greed, Population Control, Control, Going Against God, The Will of People, and more. EVERY SIN OF EACH INDIVIDUAL YOU FORCED DEATH ON, THOSE WHO HAVE DIED, AND MORE. THEIR SINS MUST BE ADDED UNTO YOU; YOUR SIN RECORD NO MATTER IF THAT PERSON IS LIVING OR DEAD. So, every sin and Sins that person – all you've subjected to your evil will have on their Sin Record, you must take on therefore, all their Sin and Sins are taken from their Sin Record and added unto you; your Sin Record. You must bare their judgement for them.

Therefore Lovey, those people must be put in a different Realm from you Lovey as their Sins are redeemed. None can face the Hell of Hell. Their Sins are cleared with Me and You Lovey but not fully and truly clear with Death because, I cannot take from Death in that way.

DARKNESS – BOOK TWO

No Lovey, I cannot allow them; these people whose Sin and Sins are cleared in our Realm of Goodness and Truth Lovey. I truly do not know their Sin and Sins, nor do I want and need to. Yes, their Sin Record is Clear but truly not clear between me and you if that makes any sense Lovey. Sind and Death. And if I am unjust Lovey, truly forgive me, and correct me and any Mistake or Sin I am making as I write now, and in the future.

As your Children and Future Generations are Cursed none can rise – they too must lose it all.

Mother Earth must now stop yielding to the lots of you.

<u>*Mother Earth cannot allow any of you to reap any good and true reward in her. If she Mother Earth disobey the CURSING OF THE LOTS OF YOU, SHE; MOTHER EARTH MUST BE MORE THAN CURSED, AND ALL LIFE TAKEN FROM HER. SHE TOO MUST BECOME UNFORGIVEN AND DEAD LIKE THE LOTS OF YOU.*</u>

Yes, you as the Wicked and Evil has and have your Death Rights that you have to live by. But, because

DARKNESS – BOOK TWO

Death did not Create Earth, Death can no longer take the goodness of Mother Earth to feed the lots of you.

Good and True Life created Earth. Now, Life is more than infinitely and indefinitely more than forever ever with end, and more than continually without end locked off and separated from all Evil as of this day forward.

Goodness and Truth, the Protection and Shield, the Blessing and Blessings of God; Good God and Allelujah must now surround, protect, and shield the Good and True of Life here on Earth.

Every goodness of God must now be taken from all evil. Death is your God therefore, go to the Realm of Death, and let Death feed the lots of you.

The Waterways of Life; Earth, the Resource of Life; Earth, the Oil Sands of Life – Earth, the Food and Foods of Life; Earth, Herb and Herbs of Life; Earth must now be taken from all Wicked and Evil Human here on Earth. God can no longer provide a home, nor can God continue to Maintain and Sustain the lots of you here on Earth. It is now forbidden.

<u>*Lovey, Mother Earth is of Good and True Life, and she must obey; comply with Good and True Life from this day forward and beyond.*</u>

DARKNESS – BOOK TWO

Yes, I am disheartened, but do you Lovey know the loathing of more than hate when I heard that disgusting more than Scum of Life Tufton tell people in Jamaica that needed water; <u>*"IF THEY TAKE THE JAB THEY WILL GET WATER."*</u>

Unforgiven Lovey because not even you can quell my true hatred for this Demon.

My son and daughter had to take their disgusting vaccines of Death. You Lovey felt the blunt of my hurt and pain with my anger. Therefore, you Lovey see just how unjust, unfair, immoral many humans are especially; Politicians and Corporate Greed – Owners and Shareholders.

<u>Everyone has a right to live therefore, I curse this demon and his family including wife, the Prime Minister of Jamaica including his Children and Wife with every curse that is known and unknown to Man – humans here on Earth, and in the Spiritual Realm.</u>

Trust me, if there was a greater Death and harsher Death greater than Great Death, I would sentence this disgusting piece of S**t, no worse than S**t including the Prime Minister of Jamaica – that Hog Andrew Holness to that hell. You do not sentence your people to death.

You do not hand your people over to Death to please your Evil Counterparts.

"DO NOT FORCE PEOPLE TO TAKE THE MARK OF THE BEAST AND SEND THEM TO THE DEPTHS OF HELL."

No Lovey, you truly do not know my Loathing and Pain for what is happening here on Earth due to the Demons' people elect to office, and the different Corporations of Death that feel the need to kill by aiding Death here on Earth.

I have a good and true need to live good and free here on Earth, and in the Spiritual Realm.

All who are good and true including me, have a right to live good and free here on Earth. Therefore, I cannot forgive any form of Evil Lovey come on now.

THE CHOICE OF DEATH IS UP TO EACH INDIVIDUAL NOT ANY POLITICAL LEADER, RELIGIOUS LEADER, NOT YOU THE CORPORATE LEADER AND OWNER, OR ANY GOVERNMENT FOR THAT MATTER.

Now look at it. The Rich is looking to Space for an escape so tell me, <u>WHAT SAY YOU THE INDIVIDUAL THAT HATH NOT MONEY TO GO LIVE IN SPACE?</u>

DARKNESS – BOOK TWO

Are you not going to be left to fend for yourself?

In all the Rich did and do to destroy all here on Earth, and you the individual helping them by buying the goods and services that were provided; were you thinking of your future, your family's future, children's future, and more?

Wow, to what's to come future wise because if you think it's rough now, you have not seen anything yet.

IF YOU AS HUMANS DO NOT CHANGE YOUR DIRTY LINEN OF SELF, YOU WILL NOT HAVE A FUTURE.

THAT WHICH GOD HAS IS FOR THE GOOD AND TRUE OF LIFE.

IF YOUR NAME IS NOT IN THE BOOK OF LIFE, YOU CANNOT BE SAVED BY GOD PERIOD.

No, the Saved cannot save you anymore because; that time is now up for billions. So truly good look to billions of you literally.

There is truly going to be rough times.

There is truly going to be more death Physically and Spiritually.

There is going to be true food shortage.
There is going to be true water shortage.

DARKNESS – BOOK TWO

More lands are going to be devoured.

Lands are going to sink, and more.

No come on Lovey. Do you see just how unjust humans have and has become?

Do you see just how vile and evil the White Race, and many in the Black Race based on hue has and have become?

Now tell me, <u>WHEN HUMANS WERE DOING ALL THEIR ILLS, DID THEY THINK OF YOU AND THE CONSEQUENCE ASSOCIATED WITH ONE SIN?</u>

In all humans were doing Lovey, <u>DID ANY TRULY AND HONESTLY THINK OF YOU?</u>

<u>*Did any think of the* SHAME AND DISGRACE THEY WERE CAUSING YOU AND SELF?</u>

Lovey, look how some Black Women are. Wow to how dem jump from Stan Pipe to Stan Pipe. You know what, let me leave it alone because; you are my good and true cause. The Wicked and Evil hath their Hell. Hell is going to be the enjoyment of all who are wicked and evil Lovey and rightfully so come on now.

Therefore Lovey, if I have completed your requirements of me good and true; let it all come to an End. Do not extend the life and time of humans here on Earth but letting Death go with their wicked and evil own no matter the race or gender.

Evil must come to an end. In all I do for you and with you Lovey, look into all I do for you, and if you find me just and fair, let all facets of evil including wicked and evil people come to an End. Let goodness and truth now reign Supreme here on Earth once again with no chance of evil – any form of Evil whether human, spirit, energy, or force get access to Earth ever again.

Michelle

DARKNESS – BOOK TWO

Is someone pregnant in my family?

I think so but there is going to be controversy.

I have this red bump under my left armpit. It does not hurt but when you touch it, it slightly hurt. Will see if it goes away.

As to who is pregnant in my family, I truly do not know because; I do not fully talk to them.

I am weird that way people. And I truly love it because, I am so not a people person in that way. I would rather stay in the background writing and unnoticed than to be in the forefront of it all.

<u>If you want to see what I look like; just pull up the Nikki Clarke Show with Michelle Jean on YouTube and you will see what I look like if you are interested.</u>

Apart from that that's it.

I truly love to write, and this is what I do.

You need to know the truth.

You need to know the difference between the Physical and Spiritual.

You also need to know that Religion cannot and will never ever save you.

I've told you in other books.

DARKNESS – BOOK TWO

"EVERY HUMAN HERE ON EARTH IS RESPONSIBLE FOR THEIR OWN SIN AND SINS."

I've also told you.

"GOD WOULD NEVER EVER LET A CHILD OF LIFE DIE TO SAVE THE WICKED AND EVIL, OR ANYONE FOR THAT MATTER."

"LIFE; GOD CANNOT BOW DOWN TO DEATH BECAUSE; LIFE AND DEATH IS TRULY SEPARATED IN THE SPIRITUAL REALM."

Therefore, *"RELIGION LIE ON GOD AS WELL AS, HAVE AND HAS DECEIVED BILLIONS."* LIFE IS NOT DEATH'S BITCH.

DEATH IS DEATH AND LIFE IS LIFE.

"THE CHILDREN AND PEOPLE OF DEATH CANNOT GO UP TO SEE GOD; FOR WHOM I CALL LOVEY FROM TIME TO TIME; WELL MORE TIME."

LIFE CANNOT GO INTO HELL TO TAKE ANYONE OUT OF HELL.

This is why I will forever ever tell you to; "look into your life, and know your Sin and Sins as well as, any Good you've done here on Earth."

<u>Absolutely no one can die to save you. That person must live and tell God to take some of their goodness to save you.</u>

The wicked and evil cannot be saved. All their Sins are recorded and any good they say they do is not looked upon as Good. All the Good they do here on Earth is looked upon as Evil; a Sin.

Evil is not capable of Good no matter how they; that person give or say they are good. From your name is written in the Book of Death, your giving here on Earth to others go on your Sin Record, and you are charged for Sin. This, a lot of people truly do not know.

<u>"GOD KNOWETH NOT YOU IF YOUR NAME IS WRITTEN IN THE BOOK OF DEATH."</u>

<u>"YOU HAVE TO FACE YOUR HELL; THE HELL YOU CREATED IN HELL FOR YOURSELF."</u>

<u>"GOD CANNOT CREATE HELL. GOD DID NOT SIN FOR YOU. YOU SINNED FOR SELF THEREFORE, YOU CREATED YOUR OWN HELL IN HELL HERE ON EARTH."</u>

DARKNESS – BOOK TWO

*Truly love **REBEL WITH A CAUSE** by Luciano, Charlie Chaplin, and Josey Wales.*

Trust me, many of you are crying now due to what I said about your hell, but you have not cried yet. Just wait until your spirit shed the flesh. Then you'll be crying; wailing to know the amount of time you will spend in the hell your created for self here on Earth as well as, what's to come shortly.

*Many of you are going to run to your god and go down on your knees and pray evil for me but know, **YOUR EVIL PRAYERS WILL NOW FALL BACK ON YOU AND FURTHER CONDEMN YOU TO HELL AND IN HELL.***

THAT EVIL PRAYER LOVEY AND OR, IF ANYONE PRAY EVIL FOR ME, MY FAMILY, AND COME AFTER ME OR MY FAMILY WITH EVIL MEANS. I AM TELLING YOU, THAT INDIVIDUAL HAVE NO FORGIVENESS FROM ME, AND THAT EVIL PRAYER AND EVIL MEANS MUST CONDEMN YOU TO HELL HERE ON EARTH AS WELL AS, IN THE SPIRITUAL REALM FURTHER LITERALLY.

God; Lovey did not tell anyone to sin. Man did.

God did not tell you to go on the Battlefield of Death to kill. Your Wicked and Evil Political Leader did, Gang Leaders did, Clergy Leader did, evil person who want and need their enemy and enemies dead did, and more. Thus, the Sin and Sins of your Political Leader, Gang Leader, Evil Person, Clergy, is added unto you. You did not think of your Spiritual and Physical Life; well being.

"THOU SHALT NOT KILL."

YOU WILLINGLY AND KNOWINGLY WENT AGAINST THE "THOU SHALT NOT KILL LAW," as written in your so-called Holy Bible.

Willful Sins and Sins knowingly done is truly not forgiven.

Now tell me, *WHAT DID THOSE PEOPLE YOU KILLED; MURDERED DONE UNTO YOU, YOUR FAMILY, YOUR GOD, AND LAND?*

And don't tell me about threats.

Look at you and your family. *What did those people you killed; murdered done unto you, your family, your god, and land?*

God gave a direct order unto humans and billions have and has broken those different laws thus, defying God and the Law and Laws given unto you.

Disobedience is a Sin.

DARKNESS – BOOK TWO

God do walk away from you when you directly disobey God, and you cannot and will never ever be saved. Your name is in the Book of Death.

You cannot go up to see God, nor can a saved save you.

Your Pastor cannot save you.
Your Imam cannot save you.
Your Deacon cannot save you.
Your Preacher cannot save you.

<u>IF ALL IN RELIGION NO MATTER THE RELIGIOUS BELIEF HERE ON EARTH RESPECTED LIFE; GOD, THEN THEY WOULD NOT LIE ON GOD. ALL WOULD HAVE THE LIFE OF GOD LITERALLY.</u>

<u>THEY WOULD NOT DISRESPECT GOD.</u>

<u>THEY WOULD BE SAVING LIVES NOT KILLING LIVES.</u>

<u>THEY WOULD DO ALL THE GOOD THEY CAN TO SAVE YOU THE PEOPLE BY ENSURING YOU ARE WALKING RIGHT, TALKING RIGHT, LIVING RIGHT, HELPING YOU IN NEED RIGHT, AND MORE.</u>

Therefore, <u>MANY USE GOD FOR PROFIT WHOOPS, PROPHET.</u>

DARKNESS – BOOK TWO

God told no one to Scam you.

No come on Lovey. People charging others for you. How does that work?

<u>YOU CANNOT CHARGE PEOPLE FOR LIFE COME ON NOW LOVEY.</u>

Now tell me Lovey; <u>WHO HAVE YOU CHARGED IN LIFE FOR LIFE, SECURITY, TRUTH, HONESTY, YOU, AND MORE?</u>

No Lovey. <u>HOW DO YOU PROFIT AND PROPHET OFF HUMANS HERE ON EARTH?</u>

No Lovey. <u>WHAT COLLECTION PLATE DO YOU HAVE HERE ON EARTH?</u>

<u>WHAT CHURCH DO YOU HAVE HERE ON EARTH LOVEY?</u>

No Lovey. <u>WHAT CHURCH DID YOU BUILD HERE ON EARTH, AND WHERE CAN I FIND IT?</u>

And Lovey, I am not being disrespectful. I know you have no Church here on Earth nor did you build any.

Wow because it is really dread here on Earth for real.

Wow to the way humans treat you bad, rob you, lie on you then; expect to have a saving grace from you Lovey.

Evil will come with a sweet tongue.

Evil do come with a sweet tongue.

It is you that disregarded Life and God.

Yes, there is repentance and or, forgiveness for some Sins but; there are no forgiveness for many.

It's almost 12:30 in the am, and I so do not want to go to sleep but; I am going to have to.

I have to walk Queenie early.

Do have a good and true day filled with many blessings.

Michelle

DARKNESS – BOOK TWO

Why do all that is wicked and evil not go to Hell and die right away Lovey?

Now Lovey, look at Artificial Intelligence.

CAN MAN OUTLIVE THE MACHINES THEY'VE BUILT?

Instead of humans doing all to preserve self, they're doing all to destroy self.

Instead of keeping Earth clean, they've done all to destroy Earth and Self.

Humans have and has caused self to become extinct.

Now Lovey, Space; the Universe cannot join the dirty bandwagon and give Evil Humans and Spirit a place to live. Hell is the home of all who are wicked and evil, and it must; have to stay this way.

Death cannot find another home apart their home in Hell.

<u>Therefore, let it be written that if Space; the Universe give Wicked and Evil Humans and Spirit; all that is Negative a home to live, then Space; the Universe must never ever be forgiven. Space and the Universe must come to an end just as Death must come to an end if the Universe join the dirty bandwagon.</u>

Darkness must cease to exist Lovey come on now.

DARKNESS – BOOK TWO

I cannot and will never ever comprehend that darkness I see the Moon coming out of.

Can humans not see this darkness Lovey because, this darkness it right there in plain sight? The Moon hide nothing from me apart from inside the Moon.

Come on Lovey you know my truth and true truth for Life. Yes, it's sad that I do not have any true waterways here on Earth that can clean my Spiritual and Earthly DNA of all its impurities including, clean and flush out all the Negatives that is in me Spiritually and Physically to never ever return.

Come on Lovey, positive and good energy that will never ever be attracted to Negative Forces, Negative Energy, Negative Spirits, Negative People, Negative Animals and Beasts, and more wicked and evil things.

Come on Lovey, there should be nothing that hinders us come on now.

The beauty of life; good and true life should never ever come at a cost to us Lovey come on now.

When I get up in the morning, I need to rise in your goodness and truth truthfully Lovey come on now.

When I am having a coffee or breakfast; I should eat with you, and have a coffee with you in goodness and truth truthfully Lovey come on now.

DARKNESS – BOOK TWO

When I go to have a shower or bath Lovey, I should bathe in your waters of goodness and truth so that all impurities in me, and on me be cleansed day in and day out.

Come on Lovey, I should be able to enjoy you here on Earth.

I should be able to talk to you face to face here on Earth.

I should be able to pick a fruit from our good and true fruit trees and give to you here on Earth.

My world, our world should never ever house any form of evil in any form or capacity come on now Lovey.

WHAT IS THE POINT OF ONLY HAVING YOU SPIRITUALLY LOVEY AND NOT PHYSICALLY?

Life is not one way; linear.

Life should encompass all who are good and true.

Life should be separated and segregated from all who are wicked and evil here on Earth just as it is in the Spiritual Realm.

Come on Lovey, I should be separated and segregated from all who are wicked and evil including separated from evil spirits, evil energy, and evil forces

DARKNESS – BOOK TWO

including, Death and the Children and People of Death here on Earth, and in the Spiritual Realm also.

The good and true and trying to be good that want to live with you void of all wickedness and evil should be separated and segregated from all who are wicked and evil including, separated from evil spirits, evil energy, and evil forces including, Death and the Children and People of Death here on Earth and in the Spiritual Realm.

Come on Lovey. <u>**Being separated and segregated from you Physically sucks.**</u>

I don't want or need to live in an unclean world Lovey come on now.

I so need to get some more candles Lovey.

Queenie is out of my bedroom for now and it feels so good.

My room is so spacious. Now I need to declutter my room.

Lovey, having so much without being able to give is frustrating. Plus, I don't want to have so much anymore. <u>*I need a true and simple life now.*</u>

No hoarding.

True giving and more good and true things.

DARKNESS – BOOK TWO

I have so much that I cannot give that it's a sin in my book. My giving is being hindered therefore, I have to stay my good and true cause in life with you Lovey. I do not need to stack up food anymore.

No Lovey, I've been stacking up on food, but my mind is truly not giving me to do this anymore.

I know I am safe and saved with you Lovey therefore, I am truly not worried about the future.

<u>You know what is so disheartening right now Lovey? Is the fact that I cannot get up and plant a seed with you good and true right now.</u>

You know what, let me not think about not being able to plant a seed with you because it hurt to the point of wanting to cry.

Life is a bitch right now Lovey. So, because I cannot plant a seed with you right now, let's have breakfast together. The breakfast and coffee I make, let us consume it together good and true. I need this this morning as this is the best I can do.

Michelle

DARKNESS – BOOK TWO

STAY AWAY by Luciano

JOURNEY by Luciano

Listen Black People, you don't have to like what I write in any of these books, but the fact is:

"WE AS BLACK PEOPLE MADE WHITE PEOPLE DEMEAN OUR BLACK GOD AND FOR THIS, I TRULY CANNOT FORGIVE."

"WE AS BLACK PEOPLE HELPED THE WHITE RACE IN MAKING OUR BLACK GOD THEIR BITCH THAT WOULD SACRIFICE A LIFE UNTO DEATH."

As Blacks, we have to stop this belief of, SACRIFICING A LIFE UNTO DEATH.

"IF GOD ALLOWED JESUS TO BE SACRIFICED ON A CROSS, GOD WOULD HAVE BEEN A MURDERER; DEATH HIMSELF."

"IF GOD ALLOWED JESUS TO BE SACRIFICED ON A CROSS, THAT WOULD MEAN GOD; THE GOD OF LIFE BOWED DOWN TO DEATH. THEREFORE, MAKING GOD WEAK, POWERLESS, AND WITHOUT A BACKBONE OR BLACKBONE BECAUSE; GOD HAD TO SUCCUMB TO THE WILL OF DEATH."

"IF GOD SUCCUMBED TO DEATH, THEN GOD AND ALL LIFE WOULD OF HAVE DIED."

"I WOULDN'T BE HERE DUE TO GOD CHOOSING ME TO TEACH YOU AS WELL AS, TRYING TO SAVE YOU FROM DEATH GOOD AND TRUE.

"GOD WOULDN'T BE HERE TEACHING YOU AND TRYING TO SAVE YOU FROM DEATH GOOD AND TRUE."

Therefore, think and know; *"THE BIBLE OF MEN – THE SO-CALLED HOLY BIBLE YOU ARE GIVEN TO BELIEVE IN, LITERALLY CONDEMN YOU TO HELL."*

From you believe in the lies of the Bible, God sever ties with you. Therefore, it is best and wise to go to God directly; not on your hands and knees, or on your knees but; sitting up on a chair, in your sofa, standing washing the dishes, sitting on your toilet, bathing, and more, and truly talk to God, and beg God for forgiveness.

Life; the True and Living God cannot bow down to Death. Nor do Death permit anyone to take from

<u>Death,</u> and I've told you this in other books as well as, in this book.

<u>Listen, when you believe God would literally BOW DOWN TO THE WILL OF DEATH, you are literally spiting in God's face.</u>

Now, go back to the Slap Naomi got in her face by that dutty stinking wretch Sonya DeVille, I told you about in Book One. <u>That disgusting and insulting slap Naomi received in her face is the same thing we as Black People do to God when we believe God would sacrifice a Child of Life; your Jesus unto Death.</u>

You are telling God, you've made God the Bitch of Death because; he had to bow down to Death by sacrificing and or, allowing Jesus to be sacrificed on a cross; <u>THE CROSS OF DEATH KNOWING ABSOLUTELY NO ONE CAN DIE TO SAVE YOU. THAT PERSON HAVE TO LIVE AND ENSURE SOME OF HIS OR HER GOODNESS GO TOWARDS SAVING YOU; THE RIGHTEOUS AND TRUE.</u>

DARKNESS – BOOK TWO

We as Black People have to stop disgracing our Black God.

We as Black People have to stop believing the lies White People tell because, they truly do not know the truth of life.

Look at it how they lie on Aliens. Have you believing in Aliens, and they truly do not know how the Spiritual Realm and Universe works.

Look at how they have you believing **MAN WALKED ON THE MOON, and you believe it without knowing that; THE MOON IS EARTH'S COOLING SYSTEM AND THE SUN IS THE HEATING SYSTEM.**

NO ONE UNCLEAN CAN HAVE ACCESS INTO, OR TO THE MOON. This I know for a fact without doubt.

I HAVE SIGHT, AND THE MOON WILL NOT GIVE ME ACCESS TO THE INSIDE OF IT BECAUSE, I AM NOT CLEAN ENOUGH. THEREFORE, NO HUMAN CAN WALK ON THE MOON. IF THEY DID, THEY WOULD HAVE LITERALLY FOUND GOD.

DARKNESS – BOOK TWO

THE BIBLE IS A TESTAMENT OF HOW FAR WHITE PEOPLE WOULD AND WILL GO WITH THEIR LIES. THEY LIED ON GOD; THE TRUE AND LIVING GOD.

THEY MADE GOD DIRTY AS THEM BECAUSE, THEY TRULY DO NOT KNOW THEIR BEGINNING; HOW THEY CAME INTO BEING.

Think many in the White Race isn't cursed; truly think again because many are cursed *just as MANY IN THE BLACK COMMUNITIES GLOBALLY ARE CURSED?*

God; the True and Living God cannot put strife between the Devil's Seed and the Children and People of Life because; *GOD KNOW NOT DEATH, NOR DO GOD KNOW THE CHILDREN AND PEOPLE OF DEATH.*

Hell; Death will never ever let the Children and People of Death; Hell reach the Realm of Life; God. Therefore, *LIFE AND DEATH IS TRULY SEPARATED IN THE SPIRITUAL REALM.*

"DEATH IS THE ONE THAT ENSURES NO ONE WICKED AND EVIL GO TO THE REALM OF GOD."

"DEATH PROTECT LIFE BY ENSURING ALL EVIL STAY IN THE REALM OF DEATH ONCE THEY GET TO HELL; THE REALM OF DEATH."

So Black People, truly know the truth because; Nations have and has been literally deceived with the *LIES OF THE DIFFERENT RELIGIONS THAT CAN BE FOUND HERE ON EARTH.*

I am going to go to bed, and we will hopefully talk some more via this book tomorrow God Willing.

EVERY MAN HAS HIS WAY by Luciano, Beres Hammond, Tony Rebel, and Louie Culture

Your life no one can live for you. Only you can live your life for you therefore, it is you that is held accountable for each sin; wrong you commit here on Earth.

If your Sins; wrongs are not forgiven, they are still on your Sin Record as debts that are unpaid. And don't think it, GOD CANNOT FORGIVE YOU OF YOUR SINS DONE ONTO YOUR BROTHER, SISTER, FRIEND, FAMILY, FOES, AND MORE.

THOSE YOU ERRED ARE THE ONES TO FORGIVE YOU PERIOD.

DARKNESS – BOOK TWO

"THE BIBLE OF MAN – MEN; YOUR SO-CALLED HOLY BIBLE IS TRULY NOT OF GOD BUT OF DEATH." You as Black People and People need to truly know this.

God cannot give dirty, nor can God give unclean come on now.

Know where you belong with God because as it is, BILLIONS HAVE NO PLACE WITH GOD RIGHT NOW. YOU ARE ALL LOCKED OUT OF THE REALM OF GOD LITERALLY.

Therefore, know your Sins versus the Good you do here on Earth literally and period.

God cannot be Death's Bitch.

It is humans that are Death's Bitch because of Sin and Sins.

It is humans that have to bow down to Death hence, the different Religions of Men that have you bowing down to Death in Prayer.

Michelle

DARKNESS – BOOK TWO

What does dreaming about a Baby Goat mean?

This Brown Baby Goat was locked in his area and someone who I did not see let the Baby Goat out. He ran so fast out of the area that he was in no one could catch him or her.

The Baby Goat ran across the street changing from Brown to Black. This White Guy was across the road, and I asked him to help me catch the Baby Goat, but he did not. I told him you let the goat out.

Suffice it to say, I did not catch the Baby Goat even when he came back and went by his and or, her mother's side. The Baby Goat's mother was Black with a white Spot on it and come to think of it, looked like a Cow. She the mother just looked at me and laid down as if she trusted me wholeheartedly.

Did I interfere with the Baby Goat when the mother laid down?

Nope, I did not want to provoke the mother due to fear, thinking the mother would hurt me if I took her child.

Was a different source connecting to me last night and or, this morning?

Yes. But this source was latching onto my creative thoughts of trying to get myself to sleep. When I wake up to go to the bathroom; going back to sleep is truly not easy for me. I have to create stories in my head in

DARKNESS – BOOK TWO

order for me to go back to sleep therefore, sleeping is hard for me on virtually all my nights.

Falling asleep again, I dreamt the same Baby Goat. The Baby Goat was caught – had a rope around its neck.

How was the Baby Goat caught?

The Baby Goat was caught in my search bar of my computer.

Weird and odd yes.

See, I am looking to promote my books to further get exposure. I was looking at Fiverr as my promotion option but after seeing that Fiverr is an Israeli Company, I can't go with that Company due to my truth and trust of Lovey; God.

I do not want or need to be hypocritical in that way.

And to be fully honest with you. Years ago, I had an account with Wix, but do not use it due that company being an Israeli Company as well.

So yes, in a way I know what the Baby Goat dream mean. I am searching for something that is truly not right for me.

Yes, I need true exposure for these books, but it is hard finding true sources that will help me promote these books, read these books, and more.

DARKNESS – BOOK TWO

<u>Word of Mouth is truly not there for me because Friends I truly do not have other than God being my true and bestest friend.</u>

If I was to tell you I had 1 particular friend apart from God that I could call and say, let's go for a coffee in an hour, I would be lying.

There's Margaret, and she is in Los Angeles. Man, we haven't talked in a while.

So, no, I am truly not a People Person in that way. I am one to run away from People due to trust. I truly do not like fake people or people who are not genuine. Truth is truly important to me, and People are truly not true.

I truly do not have a Website.

I have Instagram but Instagram do not work on your Laptop.

I do not have LinkedIn. I did shut this avenue down years ago.

I have Twitter, but do not use this avenue on a regular basis.

I have a YouTube account, but I truly do not use this avenue on a regular basis either.

I truly do not have Tic Tok.

DARKNESS – BOOK TWO

Listen, marketing and promotion is truly not my avenue. However, I've sent out books to different outlets including, Black Outlets – Magazines, but nothing substantial has and have come about this.

Yes, sent books to the Breakfast Club, but nothing has and have come of this. So, if you can be my Word-of-Mouth Promoters, Breakfast Club, True and Unconditional Reader, and more, please do the good you can to help me and you reach an international audience.

<u>Listen,</u> <u>GOD IS A PERFECT EXAMPLE OF THIS; WHEN IT COMES TO PEOPLE BEING TRUE.</u>

Humans say they love God but do all to hurt God.
Lie on God.
Use God.

Do all manner of things to discredit God, and more.

Man, the amount of dirty prayers that are sent up to God daily.

So yes, humans truly scare me because; Billions have no truth or true truth in them.

Come on Lovey humans do not look at their <u>LIFE'S PERSPECTIVE.</u>

<u>HUMANS TRULY DO NOT LOOK AT YOU, OR EVEN WONDER IF YOU FEEL PAIN.</u>

DARKNESS – BOOK TWO

<u>YOU GIVE CLEAN, BUT HUMANS GIVE BACK DIRTY IN RETURN COME ON NOW LOVEY.</u>

So, what is the point?

I truly don't know other than I truly love you.

A blessed, true, and good morning to you Lovey. It's a new day and I've walked Queenie already. She did not want to go out so early as she was complaining to me in her language, but I took her out anyway.

Lovey and God, let our day be filled with goodness and truth.

True and good Health
Wisdom
Overstanding
Good finances
Good and true Growth
Good and true Writing and Planting
Good and true You and Me all day
And more good and true things.

Certain things like this little Baby Goat going from Brown to Black, I will not worry about. As long as we are good and true to each other Lovey, let our life rise up positive, good, true, clean, balanced, harmonious, and void of all hindrance and negative forces and energy including, negative people and spirits.

It's a new day Lovey rise with me good and true.

Rise with me good and true.

DARKNESS – BOOK TWO

Unify with me good and true Lovey because I am in a Negative Cusp.

I am not doing things right, and I truly do not know why.

I am failing me.
I am failing you.

And, I truly do not know what to do.

I am racking up Sins and this is truly not good for me.

I need to purge me.
Find me.
Answer to me and yes, you.

Lovey, what is wrong with me.

I'm changing not for the good but for the negative; why?

Forsake me not Lovey because I am forsaking me.

Michelle
December 15 & 20, 2021

DARKNESS – BOOK TWO

It's December 16, 2021, and it has been an eventful day for me. Had to get a blood test done and I did something horrible that I am feeling guilty.

I so have to correct this wrong come January 2022.

Was up a bit after three am this morning playing my game, and my window is opened a bit. I could smell the air. It smelled like feces. I was hoping Queenie did not pooh in the house because I did walk her early evening. She got her usual 2 walks.

She did not pooh in the house thank God.

So, I walked her, and I could swear I saw someone walking inside the Funeral Home by the window. That was and is a first for me. I did not make anything of it. I walked Queenie and came back home and played my game yet again until it was time for me to prepare myself for my blood test.

After the test I stopped off to get a couple of things. I ordered 3 patties mild. And this is where I was wrong and sinful. Thus, the guilt that is on me right now, and plaguing me.

The young lady at the register said 2 patties. I should have corrected her and say 3, but I did not. And I've been chastising myself ever since. I did not get a bill from her to check to see if she charged me for 2 patties or 3. Now here I am in the early evening checking to see if she charged me the correct amount.

Lord have mercy. I am agonizing over $1.25 plus tax.

DARKNESS – BOOK TWO

I willingly did wrong therefore, I have to correct this wrong when I go back to that area and let them charge me an extra $1.25 so that Willful Sin can come off my Sin Record.

I am so not like this. Why I did this I cannot tell you; now to be agonizing over this.

God the agony I am in right now knowing I did something wrong.

Also, coming back from my blood test and Willful Wrong, I missed one bus. I did not feel like running for the bus so, I made it go and waited for the next one.

Getting the next bus there was Sirens in the distance and the bus driver waited until the vehicle with sirens passed. It was a Police Cruiser. Going past one traffic light the Police Cruiser was in an accident. The right side of the vehicle was totalled. There were 2 officers. 1 young Black Female, and 1 White Female. The White Female I pegged her to be Afghani, but she could have been Lebanese or something. The right side – passenger side of the vehicle, the window was smashed, the door sunken, and apart of the front fender was hanging off the car on the road. The bus driver had to radio her dispatch and tell them about the situation. She could not maneuver her bus. It was too steep as she was driving a sixty-footer bus. They had to move the truck for the bus to pass. The odd thing for me was the Young Black Police Officer who seemed casual – unphased by the accident with a smile on her face.

She and her partner did not seem hurt – they were okay.

After that, just a light up, there was a funeral procession.

Funeral Processions I truly do not like to drive by due to the dead in the casket.

So yes, today was a day for me. Thinking of those 2 lady officers, I am glad they are okay, but I cannot figure out how that crash took place because; the car had the Siren on for you to move out of the way.

The truck looked unscathed but the Police Car, wow to the destruction.

Did I dream a White Man and others trying to kill me this morning before 3am?

Yes, hence the stench of death I kept smelling thus, my eventful day. So yes, I had my lesson for the day.

And yes, I told you Willful Sins are not forgiven, but I did ask God to let 1 good that I do outweigh all of my Sins whether willfully or knowingly done or not.

As I am editing this book. On December 22, my sister called me. She was done and was going to see our brothers. I told her to pick me up and she did. I went back to the store. I picked up bread and crackers for my dad as well as, ordered two patties and the cashier, not the original cashier to charge me for 3 patties because I ordered 3 a week ago, and when the

DARKNESS – BOOK TWO

cashier said 3 patties, I did not correct her by saying I ordered 3 patties, and now I am agonizing over what I did. The cashier could not believe that I was agonizing over it. I asked her how much was one patty and she said $1.75. She told me not to worry about the 1 patty as it was Christmas. She told my sister she would charge my sister for the 1 patty next time jokingly.

So yes, I do agonize over my Sin and Sins. And yes, I did try to correct my wrong by doing the right thing. But, because it was not the original cashier I spoke to, I do not know if that wrong was corrected, and I truly do not think it was. I know it wasn't because, I did not speak to the original cashier.

For me, the beautiful part of it all was going to Lovey and telling Lovey of my good intentions and true will, and I know Lovey heard me and did not forsake me. Sins are hell for me. I don't know about you, but Sin is the pits.

I cannot feel good in myself knowing that I have done wrongs.

God wow to me and my soul; life for real.

I do worry about my soul – life all around. This is me because I truly do not want shame to follow me, or God. So yes, I am happy.

I am happy knowing that I tried to correct that wrong though you cannot correct the wrongs you have done without seeking forgiveness from the person you erred. Once forgiveness is given then that wrong is cleared from your Sin Record.

Michelle

DARKNESS – BOOK TWO

It's December 18, 2021, and my night was hell.

I did do a cover page for these books, and last night I was dreaming about the cover I did for Book One of this book.

<u>It wasn't pretty to how I saw the Moon. So, come the rest of the year and into 2022, I know it will not be pretty for humans. The Darkness surrounding the Moon is truly not good therefore, 2022 is truly not going to be pretty for humans globally.</u>

Was I dreaming about old and not so old dead people?

Yes, and they were all older White Males. Therefore, you know what; let me leave things alone because when it comes to White People, it is so not going to be good for them because; young and old is going to die in the Entertainment Industry more and more.

The dead White Males were:

Dolph Sweet and John Hoyt

I so do not want to get into the dream because it's long. In short, the dream had to do with John Hoyt being cheap; not wanting to give $20.00 to pay for gas, me and Dolph Sweet taking him; John Hoyt to the doctor. We were extremely late for John Hoyt's doctor's appointment and the Filipino Secretary that was in office filled with people did not want to let us

DARKNESS – BOOK TWO

stay for the appointment though we were late. Trust me, it did not get pretty for her, and a lot more things. So as for death in 2022, I will wait and see as, Death is being delayed for some in the Entertainment Industry until later on in the year. And you will not comprehend this but that's okay.

As for the Philippines and or, Filipinos work wise, I truly do not know.

The other actor I dreamt is George Segal. He had this light, no not light, but a round object that was white that could pass as a silver bright light.

My other dream had to do with this Black RnB and or, Soul Male Singer crushing on another Male Singer.

No, it's not Lloyd. But, wow to the Closeted Gays in the Black Music Fraternity.

Was Diddy, Beyonce, Jay Z, Trey Songz, Kevin Campbell in the dream?

Yes.

Wow to the way they were happy.

There is more to the dream like Beyonce in a onesie like bathing suit climbing over a fence.

So, because of this dream with Diddy, Jay Z plus, I know for a fact without doubt; <u>someone BLACK IS GOING TO BE SACRIFICED.</u> Thus, the Sacrifices;

DARKNESS – BOOK TWO

<u>HUMAN SACRIFICES THAT SOME IN THE WORLD DO.</u> The Abrahamic Code of Death of sacrificing Humans and Animals for fame, money, control, wealth, and more without knowing that; when you make Human and Animal sacrifices, you are taking away your life from Life, and your name must be put in the Book of Death. You cannot be saved period.

And no, a Saved cannot save you either.

<u>"THOU SHALT NOT KILL."</u>

<u>Anyone who has and have made Human, and Animal Sacrifices, are sacrificing their life, their children's life, wife's life, husband's life, and more unto Death.</u>

<u>God; the True and Living God, do not require any form of sacrifices by anyone to live.</u>

Thus, <u>"THE WAGES (PAY) OF SIN IS DEATH."</u>

So, know, if you have sold your Soul to Death here on Earth, and have as has performed your Death Ritual whether it be Sacrificing a Human, a Bull, a Chicken, Drinking Blood, bringing friends and family into the Realm of Death, and more. <u>You cannot be saved.</u> Your name is in the Book of

DARKNESS – BOOK TWO

Death and you nor a saved can redeem your Soul. That which you Willingly and Knowingly give to Death cannot be taken back. <u>You are BOUND BY DEATH PHYSICALLY AND SPIRITUALLY.</u>

And if you work Obeah, Voodoo, or Science you fall under the Abrahamic Code of Law. You cannot be saved. You are Knowingly and Willingly doing wrong. You are going against the Law and Laws of Life.

I am going to tell you this and know the truth. Do not doubt me in this. If you do, go to God and ask God for the truth if you doubt me.

<u>Now know:</u>

<u>ABRAHAM WAS NOT BLACK.</u>

<u>ABRAHAM WAS NEVER JEWISH; A JEW.</u>

<u>CAN NEVER EVER BE JEWISH BECAUSE, HE ABRAHAM PRACTICED HUMAN AND ANIMAL SACRIFICES.</u> Therefore, Abraham bowed down to Death, followed in the heritage and customs of his forefathers and mothers.

He also practiced Incest thus, making him a Family Ram. His entire family were Family

Rams. <u>THEREFORE, THEY KEPT IT ALL IN THE FAMILY.</u>

He also practiced Polygamy which is a categorical no no with God; Lovey.

<u>ABRAHAM WAS OF BABYLON.
WAS A BABYLONIAN.</u>

So, when you practice the Abrahamic Way, and live the Abrahamic Way, <u>you are LIVING AND PRACTICING DEATH'S WAY; SATAN'S WAY.</u> Therefore, you were told in Death's Book; Man's so-called Holy Bible in Revelations: <u>"woe be unto the Jews that call themselves Jews because they are of the Synagogue of Satan,"</u> and until this day Humans have not figured it out yet. Not even all in the Black Community Globally have and has figured it out yet, many say they are of God and believe in God.

Now the question I ask Blacks Globally.

Who is your God?

What God do you believe in?

Where do you stand with God with your nasty beliefs?

DARKNESS – BOOK TWO

Nasty beliefs that has and have been handed down from generation unto generation.

Nasty beliefs that many of you practice until this day.

"<u>THE NASTINESS YOU BELIEVE IN, IS THE NASTINESS YOU BECOME."</u>

Therefore, know for a fact without doubt that those who call themselves Jews are truly not Jews. They are Satan's True Evil Own thus, your Book of Death. Your Holy Bible that you say is of God without knowing that; <u>this book is Death's True Book that help you to CONDEMN YOURSELF. Yes, take you from Life – God.</u>

No, not all who say they are Jews is of Satan, but the ones you know, <u>are of THE SYNAGOGUE; CHURCHES, AND REALM OF DEATH; SATAN THUS, YOUR HOLY BIBLE.</u> King James Bible, Torah, Talmud, and more. And yes, including your ISLAMIC BOOKS like the Quran, Koran, and more.

Remember, Satan had all to Gain for Death, and Satan did gain more time for Death in Hell; Realm of Death. <u>See your Sin and Sins literally.</u>

DARKNESS – BOOK TWO

Absolutely no one in the Islamic Kingdon is of God. They too are of Death; <u>thus, they KNOW NOT ALLAH AND ALLAH KNOW THEM NOT.</u> This I know for a fact without doubt as well.

Further know:

<u>"THE CHILDREN AND PEOPLE OF GOD WHEN I ORGINALLY SAW THEM WERE ALL BLACK FEMALES WITH NAPPY AS PAPPY HAIR EXCEPT FOR 1 BI-RACIAL CHILD WHOSE FATHER WAS WHITE."</u>

Therefore, originally, <u>"THE WHITE JEWS OF THAT TIME WERE CAREGIVERS ONTO AND FOR THE CHILDREN OF GOD."</u> Therefore, not all Jews – White Jews were of the Synagogue of Satan.

So Black People, know the truth and live by the Truth of God.

<u>MUCH HAVE BEEN SAID</u> by Beresford Hammond aka, Beres Hammond

And I am so going to leave things as is because sickness was around me in the living also.

It's snowing and we've had some really warm days.

I so need an escape right now where I do not have to worry about all that is to come shortly.

All you Black People that are in Warm Lands where you can plant a little vegetables and ground provisions like, yam and banana, you are truly lucky. You have Life in the palm of your hands because, you can plant a little something, and you waste your success; blessings doing foolishness. Not all but the younger generation.

Black People, do you not know the importance of Agriculture – planting truly organic?

Black People, do you not know the importance of Water – protecting your Waterways from Evil Corporations that dump Chemical in the water to kill your good and true need and needs; Water, and Food Source?

Wow to the way many of you as Blacks do not know that you had and still have God. Yet, you as Black People and Black Leaders let evil just waltz into your country and give you their Shit of Religion, and you sup eee up fi become their Slaves as well as, the Slaves to Death literally.

Black God is real.

Black God is your true right not White Death come on now Lovey and Black People.

So, you see Lovey just how far Blacks will go to destroy their land and people for money and a true place in Hell with their God; Death.

So no, I cannot worry about Black Devils that do not seek, and do all to protect their land and lands whilst keeping the blessing and blessings of you Lovey.

I cannot worry about Black Devils that do not seek to protect self from all manner of evil Lovey come on now.

Come on Lovey. I am thinking about Ghana now and how the people of that land destroy their Land and Waterways with the different garbage of the West.

No Lovey, Africa is used and abused.

Africa is the true dumping ground for other nations. So now tell me Lovey; <u>**HOW CAN AFRICANS SAY THEY ARE BLACKS AND HAVE NOT AN OUNCE OF BLACK BLOOD IN THEM?**</u>

Africans are used as test subjects for Pharmaceutical Greed.

Africa is used as a dumping ground for Western Garbage, and more.

DARKNESS – BOOK TWO

Africans are used Religiously.

Africans have no true knowledge of life, their life, their lineage, upbringing, roots and culture, and more.

<u>ONCE YOU GIVE UP YOUR BLACK GOD, YOU ARE NO LONGER BLACK BUT; PEOPLE WHO ARE LOST, WITHOUT MERIT, A SOUL, KNOWLEDGE OF GOD, YOUR ORIGINS, LIFE, AND MORE.</u>

<u>ONCE YOU GIVE UP YOUR BLACK GOD, GOD BECOME UNREACHABLE FOR YOU, AND VIRTUALLY ALL IN THE BLACK COMMUNITIES GLOBALLY.</u>

<u>GOD SEVER TIES WITH YOU.</u>

<u>YOU HAVE TO LIVE AS THE DEAD, AND MORE FOR A TIME. WELL UNTIL GOD SENDS A SAVOUR TO SAVE THOSE WHO ARE TRYING TO BE TRUE TO LIFE; GOD.</u>

So, truly look at how the Resources of Africa is being drained by White Greed thus, <u>WHEN WHITES GAIN CONTROL OF YOUR LAND, IMPLIMENT THEIR GOVERNMENT SYSTEMS, THEY WRITE LAW AND LAWS TO SUIT WHITES WHILE DEVALUING THE ORIGINAL</u>

DARKNESS – BOOK TWO

<u>INHABITANTS OF THE LAND, AND ESURING THE PEOPLE OF THE LAND IS LEFT IN ABJECT POVERTY AS LAND AND RESOURCES IS DRAINED, AND NO LONGER OWNED BY THE INHABITANTS OF THE LAND BUT THEM; WHITES. ALL IS DESTROYED IN THE NAME OF GREED, AND THE STINKING DUTTY CREBBAY CREBBAY GOVERNMENT OF THE LAND LET THIS HAPPEN; PROTECT NOT THEIR LAND AND PEOPLE.</u>

You as Blacks cannot do as you please in your own land.

You as Blacks have to kiss the ass of your White Demonic Rulers.

You as Blacks have absolutely no say in your land because, all right and rights is literally taken from you. See the perils of Africans and South Africans including lands in the South Pacific, and Caribbean. And yes, I did differentiate South Africans from the rest of Africa. You will not comprehend this, but I comprehend it all.

So, you see Lovey, the unjust and greedy will forever ever support and protect the unjust and greedy.

Greed – the greedy will never ever think of preservation.

DARKNESS – BOOK TWO

Greed – the greedy will never ever think of future generations and preserving life for future generations.

Greed – the greedy will never ever think of Life because all they do is kill; destroy it all in the name of Death – their god, and their greed.

So, because of this Lovey, you cannot look at the Greedy of Life and In Life.

My greed for you Lovey is truly different so truly do not include my greed for you in this. I am talking about Evil Humans who live for Greed, and do all to destroy it all here on Earth like, Corrupt and Greedy Politicians, Corporations and Corporate Leaders, Religious Organizations, Religious Leaders, Gang Leaders, People, Scientist, Doctors, and more.

It's after 10am and I am going to get something to eat. My head is not feeling well.

So, as I close Book Two of Darkness Lovey, truly think of me and you, and all that is good and true for me, you, our good and true, the saved in life, and those who are truly trying to be good.

<u>If it be thy good and true will here on Earth, and in the Spiritual Realm, let no other Saviour come after me if I have fulfilled all you required of me. Truly let it all end now for all who are Wicked and Evil including, Wicked and Evil Spirits,</u>

DARKNESS – BOOK TWO

<u>*Negative Energy, Negative Forces; all that is Negative and Evil in goodness and truth Lovey.*</u>

Truly look into my anger, truth, and honesty in Book One Lovey.

Truly look into my anger, truth, and honesty in this book, Book Two Lovey.

Evil cannot continue forward in Life Lovey come on now. Evil must end, and end now.

Those who require you good and true, please let them find truth, you, and the goodness and truth in you, but never ever let anyone do to get because you know how much I more than loathe people who do to get.

<u>Curse them all that do to get literally.</u> If you have no good and true will in you to do good, then truly do not do.

True and more than unconditional love of truth to you Lovey always.

<u>*Lovey, I did say yes to your goodness and truth.*</u>

<u>*I did choose and chose goodness and truth over Death, and all that is Negative in Life here on Earth, and in the Spiritual Realm.*</u>

Never ever forget that you will always be my <u>**FOREVER YOURS**</u> good and true.

DARKNESS – BOOK TWO

Therefore, you have to be my late-night Phone Call.
Talk
Sleep
Yours good and true.

Therefore, I once again dedicate <u>**FOREVER YOURS**</u> *by D'Franco to you in goodness and in truth clean, honest, true, good, and more good and true things.*

<u>**TRAVELER**</u> *by Luciano*

Michelle

DARKNESS – BOOK TWO

BOOKS WRITTEN BY MICHELLE JEAN 2021

MY TALK JANUARY 2021

MY TALK JANUARY 2021 – BOOK TWO

MINI BOOK

JUST TALKING – THINKING

A LITTLE TALK WITH MOTHER EARTH

I NEED ANSWERS GOD

POETRY MY WAY

THE MIND AND SPIRITUALITY

I NEED ANSWERS GOD – PART TWO

MY NIGHTS

I NEED ANSWERS GOD – PART THREE

GOD IS GOOD

WHAT ABOUT US

WOW WHAT

AFRICAN – BLACK PEOPLE CUSS OUT

THE FIFTH WAVE – BLACK PEOPLE WARNING

FINAL CALL

DARKNESS – BOOK TWO

JUST MY TALK 2021

THE TRAP

CHANGES

RACIST OR NOT

GIVE ME A REASON – SPIRITUAL CLEANSING

LIFE AFTER DEATH

THE DAYS LIFE SUCKS

MOVING UP – MY HEART TO HEART WITH LOVEY – GOD 2021

DAY BY DAY

THE MARK OF THE BEAST CLARIFIED

I REFUSE

SAYINGS/POEMS 2021

I AM WOMAN

OCTOBER 2021 DREAMS

MY TALK WITH BLACK PEOPLE

NOVEMBER 2021 DREAMS

DARKNESS – BOOK ONE

DARKNESS – BOOK TWO

COMING SOON
THE HARDSHIPS OF WALKING WITH GOD

BREAK FREE/FREEDOM

Have not really sat down to fully write the HARDSHIPS OF WALKING WITH GOD *because, I don't think God want(s) me to write this book just yet or, if at all.*

Michelle